The God of Small Things

A Novel of Social Commitment

Amitabh Roy

ATLANTIC
PUBLISHERS & DISTRIBUTORS (P) LTD

ATLANTIC
PUBLISHERS & DISTRIBUTORS (P) LTD

7/22, Ansari Road, Darya Ganj, New Delhi
Tel.: +91-11-4077 5252, 2327 3880
E-mail: orders@atlanticbooks.com
Web: www.atlanticbooks.com

Reprint 2012, 2023, 2026

Published by Atlantic Publishers & Distributors (P) Ltd.

Printed & bound in India by Atlantic Print Services

Dedicated To
The 'small' people living by
the Narmadas fighting their 'small'
battle everywhere.

PREFACE

A literary work is amenable to varying interpretations and evaluations. People view it from different angles and their assessments are related to their approach. Their opinions in usual circumstances complement rather than contradict each other. But when an author is also a social activist and dares question the policies of the powerful in society, criticism often goes off track and descends to the level of calling names. Literary merits and the worth of the ideas embodied in the work are ignored in such cases. That applies to the author of *The God of Small Things* who has infuriated many known as the right as well as the left in political parlance.

Still much has been written about the thematic pattern, language, style, imagery etc. of the novel. At least four anthologies of criticism of the novel have appeared to date. The present book differs from them as it seeks to evaluate the novel sociologically. It places *The God of Small Things* with numerous socially committed novels that Indian English has produced. The world view of the author is brought to the fore and her concern for 'small things' like the neglected section of the society and environment is revealed. It shows that Arundhati Roy listens to the voiceless and reacts too.

—Amitabh Roy

ACKNOWLEDGEMENT

I express my gratitude to Professor Urmila Chakraborty whose advice, care and guidance in writing this book was immensely helpful. My father Sri Upendranath Roy is always a constant source of various thoughts and ideas to me. His scholarly help and fatherly guidance finally gave my book the present shape. My uncle Dr. Kalyan Dasgupta first presented me the copy of *The God of Small Things,* the source of all my thoughts and research works. Some journalists, human-right activists helped me a lot to come out with this small effort about the so-called "small things." All of their suggestions are really big and valuable.

Amitabh Roy

CONTENTS

INTRODUCTION

The year 1997 was an eventful one in the history of Indo-English literature. A new novelist appeared with her first novel and won the Booker before the end of the year. The attention it received from the media in India as well as abroad brought in not only showers of praise but also a lot of adverse criticism. A section of critics dismissed the novel simply with "nothing serious" while others discovered anti-Marxism, distortion of historical truth, obscenity and vulgarity in it. It was not easy under the circumstances to read it with an open mind and to judge it without fear or favour.

I had to read it several times to ascertain what the novelist meant to say and then it occurred to me that Arundhati Roy could not be dismissed lightly. She had a commitment, a social vision and anyone who failed to see that could not appreciate the novel correctly. The social commitment of the novelist held the key to several mysteries of the novel and reduced to naught most of the charges against the novel put forth by numerous critics.

The novelist has been accused of underplaying the role of the communists in Kerala for the uplift of the dalits. It is also argued that the details about Pillai and his family are not relevant to the novel. I have tried to show that Arundhati Roy analyses various social considerations that influence the members of the party. She has also connected the failings of the party to the social situation in India in general.

Arundhati Roy is supposed to have distorted the reality and presented the past as the present in respect of the dalits. The elite of Kerala boast of their liberal or progressive outlook and we are prone to take their claims at face value. The present book attempts to show that Arundhati Roy goes deep into the roots of social relationships and presents the tensions and prejudices that remain in Kerala even now.

The love-making scene at the end of the novel, according to Ranga Rao, "hangs out, an appendage, loose, wobbly. Like a camel's lip. On a Yakshi."1 To others like Abu Abraham, it is "bad enough" if not "clearly obscene."2 Parallels to it can be easily pointed out in Indian classics as well as in modern novels of the West. Sharma and Talwar concede that "its poetry and its feminist contention help to raise it from the level of mere sensationalization of sex."3 To me, it appears as a befitting reply to the "Paravan smell" both Mammachi and Baby Kochamma are worried about. It shows that nature disregards distinctions of caste and class and pleasure and satisfaction in sex relations depends on love, on willing and equal partnership only. Possibly the significance of the scene lies in its projection of love as the ultimate answer to all class and caste prejudices in society.

Then, the four-line verse in the context of the sexual abuse of Estha is alleged to be "introduced by the narrator herself for the pornographic effect."4 What the critics miss here is the truth implied, namely, that what is pleasure to one (victimize) is sometimes painful to other (victim). The novelist has frequently expressed the feelings, thoughts and words of her characters without explicitly stating so. So, the four-line verse must be assigned to the victimizer Orangedrink Lemondrink man as the context demands and all these things are related to child abuse in general in our society as the book attempts to show.

The incestuous relationship of Estha and Rahel is also objected to. Rajyashree Khusu Lahiri, who views The God of Small Things as "a taboo-breaking protest novel," finds in it an effective shock to people "out of a sense of complacency at having rid the society of discrimination based on caste and gender."5 The incestuous relationship seems to carry a message to the orthodox: if you penalise people for marrying beyond caste, religion and ethnic group, your activities may lead to the breaking of the greatest taboo, namely, incest, which is but an extreme form of in-breeding. The novelist seems to view that sex relations are purely personal matters which need not be interfered with as long as they are based on equality and consent.

Having understood the novel in this light, I have proceeded to examine Arundhati Roy as a socially committed novelist in the following pages. The first chapter discusses in brief the tradition of socially committed novels in Indian English. The second deals with the life and works (including non-fiction) of Arundhati Roy and indicates the nature of her commitment. The third chapter discusses the novelist's concern for women. It shows how the novel depicts their problems and their varying responses to them. The fourth chapter tries to reveal the novelist's concern for children; the powerless beings subjected to neglect, abuse and agony. The fifth chapter is an attempt to demonstrate how deeply the novelist has gone in analysing the sad plight of the dalits. The sixth chapter goes on to discuss the novelist's concern for the environment, a victim of human greed and callousness. Such concern seems something new in fiction to me.

The present book does not claim to be exhaustive or conclusive. As the old maxim puts it, we arrive at truth by discussion. I have attempted simply to begin that discussion in the present book.

REFERENCES

1. Rao, Ranga, "Booker of the year," *The Hindu*, Nov. 23, 1997, 8.
2. Abraham, Abu, "Breaking the Love Laws," *The Hindustan Times Sunday Magazine*, Nov. 23, 1997, 3.
3. Sharma, R.S. and Talwar, Shashibala, *Arundhati Roy's The God of Small Things—Critique and Commentary*, New Delhi, 1998, 103.
4. Ibid., 106.
5. Dhawan, R.K. (ed.), *Arundhati Roy, The Novelist Extraordinary*, New Delhi, 1999, 118.

1

THE TRADITION OF COMMITTED WRITING

We propose to study an aspect of Arundhati Roy's novel, *The God of Small Things*. Every novel, great and small, good or bad has certain elements which it cannot dispense with. Plot, characterisation, dialogue, time and place of action and style are elements obvious enough to be admitted by all. But a sixth element called criticism of life or interpretation of life or philosophy of life also creeps in invariably in a novel. It does not imply that every novelist is consciously a philosopher and writes on purpose to promote a specific view of life. What really happens is instead a complex process of sensing and expressing.

Novels devoid of a serious view of life are generally ephemeral. Mostly they do not survive their authors. To be lasting a novel requires some seriousness, depth and power. The novel must show a sound knowledge of human nature, a keen insight into motives and passions. Enduring facts and problems of life are expected to be illuminated in it. So the great novelists are not only observers of life, they become of necessity thinkers about life.

Generally people are averse to writing novels on purpose. But sometimes the novelist's concern for fellow beings leads to deep and powerful feelings and their expression gives birth to socially committed writing. We should not confuse such writing with socio-political propaganda. Novels written with a specific purpose are generally failures because the attempt to write a good story and to make out a case at the same time is too difficult but great novelists have written on purpose and their attempts have not only succeeded but brought glory to them.

Harriet Beecher Stowe (1811-56) is an instance to the point. She wrote her novels *Uncle Tom's Cabin* (1852) and *Dred, a Tale of the Great Dismal Swamp* (1856) on purpose. She was an opponent of the institution of slavery that prevailed in the United States of America at the time. She exposed the inhuman nature of the institution in her novels and expressed deep concern for its victims who were brought to America from Africa in chains, exploited and killed with impunity. The first of these novels was a "sensational success" (as Mercus Cunliffe puts it in *The Literature of United States,* Penguin, 1986, p. 28) and contributed to mobilising public opinion against the slavery which culminated in the Civil War and abolition of that vile institution. The universal appeal of her novels keeps them afresh even now.

Arundhati Roy's novel like the rest of its kind has all the usual six elements in it, but it is a socially committed writing at the same time. Arundhati Roy has read several western novels and she is undoubtedly influenced by them. But so far as her social commitment is concerned, it is rooted in the Indian soil. Her novel is not an imitation of some western model in this respect. She has behind her a long and rich tradition of socially committed writing in Indo-Anglian novels. It is relevant here, therefore, to have a look at this tradition and discover her roots.

Novel writing in English in India began (in the modern sense of the term) not earlier than the later part of the nineteenth century. That was but natural because creative writing in English required education in English. Though the British East India Company had virtually become the sovereign power in India by 1764 (the battle of Buxer) and it had introduced limited instruction in English for its own purposes in Bengal, Madras and Bombay, it was yet to spell unequivocally its policy about education in the areas under its control. That occurred on March 7,1835 as the Council under Governor-General William Bentinck passed a Minute on education making English the medium of instruction in Government subsidised schools. That, in effect made English the official language of British India.

English exposed Indian intellectuals to the ideas of Mill, Spencer and Bentham on the one hand and made them aware of the socio-political changes that were taking place in Italy, Germany, Russia, Japan etc. on the other. But no less important was the fact that they became acquainted with the literary tradition of the West in general and of England in particular. That is what generated a demand for novels not only in English but in regional languages as well. Inevitably, India produced its own novelists very soon.

The early novels in English written in India, to put them chronologically, are the following mainly. Excluded from this list are the works which though published later in English were originally written in Bengali or some other regional language:

> *Rajmohan's Wife* by Bankim Chandra Chatterjee (1864); *The Hindu Wife* by Rajlakshmi Devi (1876); *Bianco* by Toru Dutta (1878); *Roshinara* by Kali Krishna Lahiri (1881); *Bijoy Chand* by H. Dutt (1888); *Kamala, A Story of Hindu Life* by Mrs. Krupabai Satthianadhan (1894); *Saguna, A Story of Native Christian Life* by Mrs. K. Satthianadhan (1895); *Sarata and Hingana* by Khetrapal Chakrabarti (1895); *Padmini* by T. Ramakrishna (1903); *The Slave Girl of Agra* by Ramesh Chandra Dutta (1909); *Nurjahan* by Sir Jogendra Singh (1909); *The Lake of Palms* by Ramesh Chandra Dutta (1909); *Nasrin* by Sir Jogendra Singh (1915).

As Uma Parameshwaran rightly observes, the English educated in the earliest epoch "responded actively to certain kinds of English literature and philosophy, such as romantic idylls, philosophical treatises, idealistic outpourings, re-enactments of history. This accounts for their interest in Scott, Dickens, Wordsworth, Carlyle, Ruskin and Macaulay, and their imitation of them."[1] In case of the novels, Walter Scott seemed to offer them the perfect model with a combination of story telling and nostalgia for an idealized past.

However, it would be a gross error to assume that the nostalgia was merely a product of imitating Scott. There seems to be a general tendency in human mind to seek the golden age in the past. Thus the Greeks, according to the testimony of Hesiod, believed that there had been four ages—"golden, silver, bronze and iron—each worse than the one preceeding."[2] People in Ancient Persia and India too had a cycle of ages associated with the idea of progressive decline.[3] Babylonians and the Jews did not differ in essence. *The Book of Daniel* in the *Old Testament* refers to the succession of the ages.[4]

Apart from this general tendency of the human psyche, we find a historical explanation for the nostalgia. While the Christian missionaries and a section of the white elite were trying arrogantly to misrepresent the past of India, there were also scholars who rated it high. We are well aware of what Goethe wrote on reading the translation of Kalidasa's *Sakuntala*. Humboldt found in the *Bhagavadgita* "perhaps the deepest and loftiest thing the world has to show." Arthur Schopenhauer discovered "the highest human wisdom" and "almost super human conceptions" in the *Upanishads*.[5] Louis Jacolliot wrote a book *La Bible dans L'Inde* which appeared in English in 1870. He called India "the cradle of Humanity" and argued that all the main currents of thought in the world were derived from India.

There is little wonder then, that the past lured the early novelists. T. Ramakrishna's *Padmini* is a story of a tyrant king's love for Padmini who rejects him in favour of the impoverished but noble Chennappa. This historical romance enshrines the memory of the Vijayanagar Empire and the battle of Talikote in 1565 which brought an end of that empire. R.C. Dutt's *The Slave Girl of Agra,* Sir Jogendra Singh's *Nurjahan* and K.K. Lahiri's *Roshinara* are the novels that take us back to the days of the Mughal rule. Such novels have "for us today no more than an antiquarian or historical interest."[6] But the nostalgia continued even after 1947 and produced remarkable novels like Vimala Raina's *Ambapali* (1952) and A.S.P. Ayyar's *Chanakya and Chandragupta* (1952).

But we observe another tendency too in Indian English novels from the very beginning. That is the tendency to notice social life and to reflect upon it. That was but natural at a time when Indian society was subjected to ruthless criticism by the Christian missionaries and the western education had brought in liberal bourgeois ideas about human relations. The elite as a result became aware of the weaknesses of Indian society like superstitions, early marriage, polygamy, the miserable condition of the women in general and widows in particular and the excesses of caste system. So, the early novels are not entirely devoid of social criticism and protest.

Ramesh Chandra Dutt's *The Lake of Palms* (1909) is the most daring of these novels. It is based on the social life in Bengal toward the end of the nineteenth century and its action culminates in the marriage of the young widow Sudha to Sarat. S.K. Ghosh's *The Prince of Destiny: The New Krishna* (1909) seeks to synthesize the best in the East and West to invigorate the society. Sir Jogendra Singh's *Nasrin* (1915) exposes the self-indulgence of the Nawabs and Talukdars, the relics of the feudal society.

While the social awareness of such novels cannot be denied, Indian English witnessed an unprecedented growth of socially committed writing by the 1930s. There were several developments during 1920s that left their mark on Indian history. The leadership of the national movement passed on to Mahatma Gandhi during the decade and Indian National Congress, which was deemed no better than a group of petitioners to the British Government, began to involve the masses for the first time. His ideas called Gandhism had an unquestionable wide appeal. Then, as the Bolsheviks in Russia were able to overcome foreign aggression, civil war and famine and began to lay the foundations of a new economy, Marxist or apparently Marxist ideas came in. They had a pronounced impact on creative writing as Progressive Writers' Association came into being.

That our choice of the 1930s is not arbitrary is borne out by the fact that William Walsh marks it as the age of "genuine novelists." According to Walsh, "the art of fiction was an end in itself and not just a means for communicating other kinds of truth."[7] It was "they who defined the area in which the Indian novel in English was to operate, drew the first models of its characters and themes and elaborated its particular logic."[8] Walsh names three of these "genuine novelists"—Mulk Raj Anand, R.K. Narayan and Raja Rao—and strangely enough, the first one of them turns out to be a socially committed novelist by faith.

Mulk Raj Anand was born in Peshawar in 1905. His father belonged to a family of traditional coppersmiths but served in the Indian Army for living and became a Subedar in course of time. His mother came of sturdy peasant stock. Educated at Lahore he went to London in 1924 with the encouragement and material support of the poet Iqbal, his college principal and his mother. He completed his education in London and Cambridge. His thesis on *Bertrand Russel and the English Empiricists* won a Doctorate in Philosophy in 1928. Though his academic attainments might have made him a Professor in some college or university, he chose the hazardous profession of creative writing. He lived in England for 21 years, though he visited India occasionally. Now, he is living in Maharashtra near Khandala Railway Station. He has got more than one hundred medicinal plants in his compound and treats ailments like cold, diseases of eye, diabetes etc. with them.

Anand was involved with the Unity Theatre and Left Book Club in England. He was also associated with Progressive Writers' Association (founded in 1935) in India. Such involvement and association has left its mark on his views about art. Thus he declares bluntly: "All art is propaganda. The art of Ajanta is propaganda for Buddhism. The art of Ellora is propaganda for Hinduism. The art of the Western novel is propaganda for humanity against the bourgeoisie. Gorky as a humanist dared to speak of man, man's condition, not to say how awful it is, but he also suggested what man could be. And thus he did propaganda for man."[9]

Thus he presents himself as a humanist, an admirer of Gorky and therefore also of the ideas of "socialist realism." As for his fiction, it is exclusively concerned with India. He writes about the poor and deprived in the villages, the miserable conditions of the untouchables and urban toilers, the sad plight of the women and the orphan, and the cruelties of caste. Iyengar, referring to the artistic perfection and themes of his novels, makes a significant remark: "The craftman's industry, and meticulous attention to detail and the army man's dare-devilry and feeling for adventure are among the major constituents of Mulk Raj Anand's heritage from his father. From his peasant mother he doubtless derived his common sense, his sense of the ache at the heart of Indian humanity and his understanding compassion for the waifs, the disinherited, the lowly, the lost.[10]" His "angry reformist way" leads Walsh to find in him "a less humourous Dickens and a more emotional Wells."[11]

Mulk Raj Anand is a prolific writer. He has written a lot including fiction and non-fiction both. His novels in chronological order are the following: *Untouchable* (1935); *Coolie* (1936); *Two Leaves and a Bud* (1937); *The Village* (1939); *Across the Black Waters* (1940); *The Big Heart* (1945); *Seven Summers* (1951); *Private Life of an Indian Prince* (1954); *The Road* (1961); *Death of a Hero* (1963); *Morning Face* (1976); *The Bubble* (1984) etc. The first three of these novels appeared "like so many packets of dynamite" to the bureaucracy. They were banned in India and even in England, *Two Leaves and a Bud* had to be withdrawn from circulation on the threat of persecution as an obscene book. As space does not permit us to discuss all his novels here, we confine our discussion to the first three novels only.

Untouchable is the "most compact and artistically satisfying" of all according to Iyenger.[12] It is shortest of all. Describing a day in the life of the sweeper boy Bakha in the town of Bulashah, Anand admirably preserves the unities as in a classical play. The eighteen year old boy Bakha, one of the sons of the Jamadar Lakha, has a fascination for western dress, for military uniform. Obviously, he loves to live in a clean and decent way. But born in a society, segmented into castes, sub-castes and outcastes and belonging to the lowest rung of society, he lives in out castes' colony and his job is to clean latrines. His sister, Sohini, fetches water from the caste well which depends on some gentleman "taking pity on her and giving her the water" she needs. The other thing she has to do outside is to collect bits of bread at the houses of the well-to-do.

During the course of his usual toil, Bakha touches a caste Hindu and he is slapped for it by the latter and subjected to the most inhuman treatment before a crowd. That makes him aware of his place in the society and immediately after the slap scene, he observes an old Hindu touching a bull and reflects critically on it. Then Bakha learns how the priest, Kalinath had attempted to molest his sister Sohini. That enrages him but his clenched fists soon relax and fall loosely by his side. He realises his utter inability to retaliate. His father, Lakha, is less sensitive and accepts untouchability in a fatalistic manner. Lakha asks him "you didn't abuse or hit back, did you?" and Bakha replies: "No, but I was sorry afterwards that I did not." While untouchability is the destiny with the old man even though bitter, it is a curse to be fought and destroyed to the young man.

Bakha spends the afternoon in the company of his friends including Ramcharan, the washerman's son and Chhota, the cobbler's son besides 'attending' the marriage of his friend Ramcharan's sister, a girl Bakha appreciated but could not marry as she belonged to a higher caste. Havildar Charat Singh treats Bakha kindly disregarding his caste and gives him a new hockey-stick. The hockey play in the evening leads to a free fight and injures a little boy. As Bakha tries to lift the injured, the boy is polluted according to his mother. When the poor fellow returns to his home, he is scolded for idling away all the afternoon and driven out of the house.

Thus we find that the boy is treated worse than an animal because of his caste. Chapatis are flung down to him from the third floor, jilabis are thrown at him as a bone is thrown at a dog and touching a caste Hindu even inadvertently incurs wrath and abuse. The caste Hindus, referring to people of his caste, declare in a callous, dictatorial manner: "They ought to be wiped off the surface of the earth." As Bakha sums up his experiences: "They think we are mere dirt because we clean their dirt." The worst thing about it is that his father fails to share his feelings due to the generation gap.

The novel does not end without some suggestions to solve the problem of the untouchable. Bakha finds three options before him. Colonel Hutchinson, the salvationist, asks him to convert to Christianity and end his caste. Then as he listens to the speech of Mahatma Gandhi at a public meeting, he finds something new, encouraging as well as disturbing in it. Mahatma Gandhi declares untouchability "the greatest blot on Hinduism," calls the untouchables the men of god, prefers to be reborn as an outcaste rather than a caste Hindu and dismisses all talk about pollution as satanic. Finally the hero encounters the poet Iqbal Nath Sarshar (obviously a prototype of the author himself) who dreams of "a casteless and classless society" and argues that the introduction of a modern sanitary system—the flush—can remove the stigma of untouchability and bring freedom and dignity to the sweepers. Impressed by what he has learnt, Bakha returns to his father to tell him about the Mahatma and the machine.

E.M. Forster thought very highly of the novel and wrote a preface to it. The novel seemed "indescribably clean to him" and had "gone straight to the heart of the subject." Walsh detects in Anand "the habit of preaching at the reader" but has to conclude that "when his imagination burns and the dross of propaganda is consumed...there is no doubt that he is a novelist of considerable power."[13] The portrayal of the social milieu in the novel is so accurate that "*Untouchable* strikes us as the picture of a place, of a society, and of certain persons not easily to be forgotten."[14] It is an indictment of a decadent and perverted orthodoxy and yet it does not come to us as a sermon as the novelist has succeeded in identifying himself with the hero totally. Rightly does Saros Cowasjee remark: "So strong indeed is the identification with his hero that for the best part of the novel we forget the presence of the novelist."[15]

Coolie is about twice as long as *Untouchable* and covers several years and a large space. While caste system is the oppressive, victimizing force in the first novel, the second shows the tyranny of money. Perhaps Anand wants to show that one can survive the tyranny of caste, but not the oppression of money that destroys the poor. *Coolie* too, like *Untouchable*, is an indictment of society as a whole. Swiftness and diffusion characterise the novel and a "mixture of the horrible and holy, the inhuman and the humane, the sordid and the beautiful" is presented to us which makes it so close to actuality. Iyenger rightly remarks: "If *Untouchable* is the microcosm, *Coolie* is more like the macrocosm that is Indian society."[16] P.K. Rajan finds "a unity of both a naturalistic representation of the brutal face of capitalism and a romantic lament for the tragedy of innocence."[17] To Marlene Fisher, the novel brings "a sense of movement and its attendant color and restlessness—not only of Munoo, but of all India."[18]

The action in the novel *Coolie* covers less than two years in the life of a waif who belongs to Kshatriya caste. The boy, Munoo is fourteen when the story begins and just sixteen when he dies at the end of the novel. The novel is divided into five chapters, each depicting a particular phase of his life. The first chapter shows his life in the idyllic valley of the Kangra Hills. The poor orphan is compelled to live with his uncle Dayaram and aunt Gujri but their ill treatment causes him to flee. In the second chapter, we find him employed as a domestic servant in a bank clerk's household. Babu Nathoo Ram's house at Sham Nagar proves a mad house, a prison to the boy. People in that house are unhappy and cruel and Bibiji is the worst of them. Chota Babu, who is disposed to be happy and give happiness to others, is the sole exception. The harrowing experiences in the house prompt him to ask himself: "Who am I—Munoo? Why am I here in this house?" He thinks further and comes to the conclusion: "No, caste does not matter...there must only be two kinds of people in the world: the rich and the poor." Beaten mercilessly at the house, the "ineffectual pawn on the chessboard of destiny" rebels and runs away. The third chapter deals with his life at Daulatpur. As Munoo left the house of Babu Nathoo Ram, he sought his temporary refuge in a train where a passenger discovers him lying under the bunk and takes him to Daulatpur. He works there first in the pickle factory of Prabha and after the collapse of his business, he serves as a coolie in the city market and as a porter at the station. The fourth chapter shows his experiences in Bombay. Accidently he has become acquainted with an elephant trainer in a circus who helps him to reach Bombay. There he experiences the life on the pavements and slums and serves at Sir George Cotton Mills. There he witnesses the exploitation of the "dried up, shivelled, flat footed, hollow-chested, hollow-checked, hollow-eyed" workers, 'labour trouble,' Hindu-Muslim disturbances and all the excesses and corruptions of the colonial rule. As he runs up Malabar Hill to escape the hectic police action, he is knocked down by a car. The owner of the car Mrs. Manwaring takes him to Shimla. The fifth chapter describes Munoo's life in Shimla. As Munoo felt like a trapped animal in Bombay, weak and helpless, he went to Shimla to serve as a servant and rickshawpuller of Mrs. Manwaring. He dies there of consumption.

While *Untouchable* is akin to the lyrical and *Coolie* has almost epic quality, *Two Leaves and a Bud* is essentially a dramatic novel that culminates in a tragedy. Gangu, a victim of poverty and money-lenders leaves his village near Hoshiarpur in the Punjab lured by Buta Ram, the cunning agent of the tea-planters. The middle aged peasant and his family comprising his wife Sajani, their fourteen year old daughter Sheila and seven year old son Buddhu are inveigled into indentured labour on the British run Macpherson Tea Estate in Assam. There Gangu discovers that he has landed from the frying pan into the fire. The white man's plantation proves a prison: "The prison has no bars, but it is, nevertheless an unbreakable prison." The coolies are treated as beasts of burden and have to live in damp, dingy huts infested with germs. They are subjected to graft, usury and exploitation both by Indian agents and their British masters. Though the work is hard, the payment is poor. While he earned eight annas a day in his village, he is paid only three annas for him, two annas for his wife and daughter and three pice for his child. Soon Gangu has an attack of malaria and then his wife Sajani dies of cholera. Gangu seeks a loan to cremate his wife but the planter Mr. Croft-Cooke not only refuses to advance a loan but kicks him brutally for breaking the quarantine regulations. Then, as two coolie women quarrel, the assistant manager Reggie Hunt orders a brutal suppression by the sardars which injures some coolies. The aggrieved coolies march peacefully to the Burra Sahib seeking redressal of their grievances. The march is dispersed forcibly and the army is called out to deal with the situation. Gangu is now fined rupees fifty on the charge of having led the march. But that too is not the end of his misery. While Sheila is plucking the tea leaves alone, Reggie Hunt approaches her intending to molest her but she runs away followed by the brute. Reggie's attempt to rape the girl is foiled but Gangu is shot dead by the villain. A trial follows but the criminal is acquitted by Justice Mowberley who concurs with the majority view of the jury—consisting of seven Europeans and two Indians and finds the accused 'not guilty' of charges of murder and culpable homicide.

The character of Gangu is far from heroic. He suffers a series of misfortunes and atrocities as part of his destiny. But his instinct eggs him on to rebel at times. So, we read in the novel: "The indifference of fatalism in him, which had sprung not so much from a belief in God, but from years of suffering seemed to give place for a moment but to homicidal fury which glistened with the spirit of retaliation."

But he can not stick to that position for long. Soon he "agrees to pay the fine of rupees fifty and accepts everything else without even so much as a gesture of complaint." He cries helplessly: "Lord, God, deliver me. Save me from the wrath of my enemies. My wife is dead! My children are young! And my heart is weeping!" Such oscillation between anger and despair is a product of endless poverty and suffering which forces people to submit to their lot. It also demonstrates the helplessness of the individuals before the system.

Despite his dislike for the British rule and the exploitation it perpetuated, Anand as a humanist could not blacken all the white folk and make all the Indian characters good. So we find notorious people like agents, sardars, money-lenders among Indians. Among the Europeans, Reggie Hunt is not only a melo-dramatic villain but a representative of the brutal power of colonialism and capitalism which destroys human values. But the novelist, like a pathologist, studies his case patiently and reveals the roots of his cruelty. Counterpoised to Croft-Cooke and Reggie Hunt is John de la Havre, the doctor, who shows utmost sympathy for the Indian cause and joins the march of the coolies. He is dismissed summarily and his romance with Barbara, the daughter of Croft Cooke comes to an abrupt end. If the white man Havre loses his job and love for his sympathies with the poor and the oppressed, the villain Reggie Hunt finds not a single sympathiser among his own people. So we find that the system spares none. The novel seems to endorse Havre's contention: "It is no use hating anyone.... It is the system, you must hate the system."

We notice that in these three novels Anand shows a deep social awareness and exposes a system that enables the powerful and the rich to oppress the weak and the poor. Reggie becomes a powerful symbol for racial, social and sexual harassment and oppression. Arundhati Roy follows Anand's concern for the victims of caste and class oppression. Velutha is an untouchable and belongs to the working class. His lot is not much different from that of Bakha, Munoo and Gangu. Like the heroes of Anand, Velutha too finds himself helpless before a system based on inequality and exploitation. A tea garden in Assam and a pickle factory in Kerala provide the background of casteist and sexual exploitation of the powerless by the powerful in her novel. Thus her novel blends together certain traits of the three novels of Anand in it and reminds us of Anand's books.

Dr. Bhabani Bhattacharya is the other novelist who deserves mention as a socially committed novelist. A much translated novelist, he got the Sahitya Akademi Award in 1967 in recognition of his standing and achievement in the field of Indian fiction in English. His novels in the chronological order are: *So Many Hungers* (1947), *Music for Mohini* (1952), *He Who Rides a Tiger* (1954), *A Goddess Named Gold* (1960), *Shadows from Ladakh* (1966) and *A Dream in Hawaii* (1978). He does not seem to have any politic ideological affiliations but the first three of his novels show a deep concern for the suffering humanity and a keen eye for social problems.

The first novel, *So Many Hungers* (published in October, 1947) narrates the woeful story of the famine of 1942-43, a man made disaster that took a toll of two million people in Bengal. Unscrupulous people like Samarendra Basu and Sir Lakshminath of Bengal Rice Limited store foodgrains and make money, common people are forced to starve. The conditions worsen after the mass arrest of political leaders following the 'Quit India' resolution. Ruthless suppression and atrocities, indiscreet firing and victimization of the masses bring in a reign of terror. A man lighting the street lamps in Calcutta is mistaken for a political activist and shot dead. Kajoli's husband is shot dead for no reason while hurrying to the railway station.

In the name of security measures more than forty thousand boats are snatched away from the fishermen and burned. Thus the fishermen are deprived of their living. Coastal villages are evacuated under the same pretence. The victims know the falsity of the government's excuse but they are helpless. Then hoarders, profiteers and black-marketeers are let loose by the authority. The unholy alliance of the government and traders compels the peasants to sell all their rice at a nominal price. Later, the peasants have to buy it in black market at a ten times price. The rice hunger begins as a thin stream but swells soon into a mighty flood. Rice, the common staple food, becomes a rare luxury to them and they have to sell their belongings for a handful of rice. They sell their land, cottages and cattle and become uprooted. Inflation has reduced the worth of their money to nothing, so they get little even by selling all their belongings.

The flow of destitute then rushes to Calcutta which has its own limitations. Counterpoised to the hunger for food on the part of the poor is the wealthy men's hunger for sex. So brothels prosper and peasant girls are forced to prostitution. Even Kajoli, the daughter of a freedom-fighter peasant finds no alternative to save her mother and younger brother. A fisherman, unable to bear the sight of her child's hungry, blank stare and having no milk to feed the child, buries the baby alive. Then there are pathetic scenes like Onu eating bits of food from garbage and a baby suckling the breast of its dead mother. Kajoli's mother commits suicide as she does not like to be a burden on her already starving children. Such things happen despite fair harvest and during a war that was supposed to be fought for democratic and human values.

As Iyenger remarks: "*So Many Hungers* is no doubt an impeachment of man's inhumanity to man, but it is also a dramatic study of a set of human beings trapped in a unique tragic predicament."[19] There may be people who think that the novel has become dated now as the British have left and famine seems to have become a thing of the past. Unfortunately, however, hoarders, profiteers and black marketeers have not disappeared. Attempts to create false scarcity of salt, sugar and mustard oil are not unknown to us. The roots of the tragic predicament narrated in the *So Many Hungers* are still there in our society and we have to beware of them. That is the relevance of the novel to our own times.

His second novel *Music for Mohini* highlights the differences between the orthodox, tradition-bound village life and the semi-westernised life of the city and the problem it poses before women sometimes when they move to a different environment after marriage. Rooplekha, a village-bred but city-wed girl had to stand the critical stare of the sophisticated when she went to live with her husband in the city. A similar problem of adjustment arises when Mohini, a Calcutta-born popular radio artiste marries Rooplekha's scholarly brother, Jayadeva and goes to his village, Behula. Such girls, "pulled up by the roots," become victims of their own choice and have to suffer a lot. But the novelist does not take a negative view of it. As Rooplekha puts it, such marriages "serve some real purpose," they make "a bridge between two banks of a river." Mohini realises that somehow she has to synthesize the old and the new, the country and the city. Mohini, the artiste, knows well that music is a matter of harmonising different notes and proceeds to accomplish it in her own life. The title of the novel is significant as it describes how she succeeds in creating music for herself in life. We notice that in this novel the novelist concentrates on the problems of women.

The third novel, *He Who Rides a Tiger* takes us back to the days of Bengal famine. "Less sombre in its hues than *So Many Hungers,* the indictment it carries is delivered with more deftness, and satire and entertainment are mixed in almost equal proportion."[20] Kalo, an honest blacksmith contented with his profession, is uprooted from his town and moves to Calcutta. He feels hungry and attempts to steal banana from a first class compartment. He has eaten nothing for days and so he cannot help it. But the magistrate does not care and punishes him with three months rigorous imprisonment. This happens at a time when despicable crimes of jute merchants, rice merchants and other rich people involved in immoral traffic go unnoticed and unpunished. In prison, he experiences the tyranny of the warden and comes out an embittered man.

Released from jail, he joins the flux of hungry men in Calcutta. But his efforts to survive honourably bear no fruit. He helps the Corporation gang in removing dead bodies from streets and gets just one rupee a day which cannot keep him alive. Then he becomes a pimp. To his great shock, one night he finds his only daughter brought to one of the harlot-houses. He rescues her just in time but she carries a stigma which is difficult to forget. So, Kalo resolves to avenge injustice done to him by the alliance of 'caste and cash.'

So Kalo the blacksmith becomes Mangal Adhikari the brahmin overnight and a 'miracle' takes place. A stone Shiva rises from the ground and a temple is built around it. Fraud pays rich dividends where honesty had made even survival difficult. Both riches and honour are now showered upon him and he receives them jubilantly. The novelist explains his psychology behind the behaviour as follows: "It was not just a question of living. It was a question of revenge. We've got to hit back. Through what better means than Temple? And let their proud women, limbs draped in jewels and chastity, bow down to a girl who had almost fallen."

Even amid this drama of lies and deception, Kalo shows his best human qualities. Instead of casting into the Ganga the buckets of milk donated by the devotees for the idol's bath, he manages to divert the same after bath for feeding hungry children. His devotees include all the rich of Calcutta and even the magistrate who had sentenced him for a petty offence, comes to him and touches his feet humbly.

But his satisfaction is not everlasting. Prosperity does not pacify his conscience. He feels alienated from his former self. His daughter, Chandralekha too longs for the former days to return as their new life is simply suffocating. Her role as the Mother of Seven-fold Bliss, an object of adoration, brings no pleasure to her. So both father and daughter are increasingly ill at ease. Kalo buys a blow-pipe and tools and runs a smithy in the upper chamber of the temple secretly but as the smoke leads to suspicion, he has to give up the attempt. Various complications arise in his life and he feels like a man riding a tiger who does not know when to stop and how.

At last, Kalo gathers courage and reveals the whole truth before a big assembly. That shocks and enrages the audience but brings utmost solace to Kalo and his daughter. Purged of the lies and deceptions of the past fully, they feel contented to begin their life anew, a modest and truthful life.

Thus, *He Who Rides a Tiger* is powerful indictment of the society that perpetuates superstitions, corruption, injustice and degradation of the human race. It shows that a system that makes life unbearable to the poor and honest and rewards the rich and dishonest cannot but breed charlatans and cheats. It also demonstrates that human beings are not basically mean, unkind and deceitful. Only a section of them is led by baser instincts, the majority of them are compelled to do things which are unbecoming to them simply for the sake of survival. The latter cannot resist the pricking of their conscience which compels them to return to the path of virtue sooner than later. That is why the novel remains relevant to us even after the disappearance of the British and the famine.

We can connect Arundhati Roy's novel with several themes in Bhattacharya's work. In *So Many Hungers,* human beings are shown starving to death. The hunger in *The God of Small Things* is more deep-rooted and therefore more palpable. Baby Kochamma starves of love as she cannot marry the man of her choice. Mammachi married to a wife-beater finds little solace in life and her son who saves her from that brutality proves no better than a usurper. Margaret who comes to Ayemenem in search of relief, loses her only daughter. Ammu's quest for love destroys her own life as well as that of her lover. Children in the novel are also deprived of parental love and the company they need. Thus her novel depicts a sort of famine which leaves people starving emotionally.

Like the heroine *of Music for Mohini,* Ammu and Rahel in Roy's novel attempt to adjust themselves to different environment. They fail while Mohini succeeds because the couple in Bhattacharya's novel understand their partner better than their counterpart in Roy's novel.

Corresponding to the cheats and charlatans of Bhattacharya's *He Who Rides a Tiger,* we find people like Pillai, Chacko and Mathew in Roy's novel who talk high and act low. Like Bhattacharya, Roy too indicts the system that degrades human beings on the ground of caste and sex and perpetuates exploitation, injustice and violence. Like Bhattacharya, Roy too believes in the basic goodness of human beings.

Khuswant Singh, the next socially committed novelist we discuss, was born in the Punjab in 1914. As *India Today* put it, he is a "man for most professions—he's been a lawyer, bureaucrat, editor (*The Illustrated Weekly, The Hindustan Times* and *Yojana*), academic (taught at Princeton), scholar and Rajya Sabha member."[21] He is a queer person in as much as he appears paradoxical. He has translated the Japji and other religious writings and yet he is not religious. He "rejected religion from the age of 25." As a secular nationalist, he had the courage to call Bhindrawale a homicidal maniac; but the consciousness of his Sikh identity forced him to give up the Padma Bhusan after Operation Blue Star.[22] He has written a scholarly work, namely, *History of the Sikhs* which is likely to attract scholars for a long time. And still he is better known for his controversial statements (about Tagore, literature in Indian languages, Sahitya Akademi etc.) and jokes.

His joke-books have brought him more popularity than anything else. Thus, he has a non-serious image. Girish Karnad, the Kannada playwright rightly remarked: "His non-serious image has always come in the way of his assessment as a novelist."[23] Sobha De, who co-authored with him an anthology *Uncertain Liaisons* has a similar opinion about him and regrets that "others tend to take him not seriously."[24] This best-selling author of over 80 books has written two remarkable novels *Train to Pakistan* (1956) and *I Shall Not Hear the Nightingale* (1959), the first one of which is not only serious but contains an admirable blend of social awareness with artistic perfection.

Train to Pakistan is a novel about the disaster that followed in the wake of the partition of India in 1947. Many Indian writers have focussed on the same theme in English and regional languages. B. Rajan's *The Dark Dancer*, Balwant Singh Anand's *Cruel Interlude*, Attia Hossain's *Sunlight on a Broken Column*, Manohar Mulgaonkar's *A Bend in the Ganges*, Raj Gill's *The Rape* and Chaman Nahal's *Ajadi* are the most famous in English among them. *Aur Insan Mar Gaya* by Ramanand Sagar is also well-known among the novels published in Indian languages. But *Train to Pakistan* surpasses them all in artistic excellence and stark realism and "trenchant exposition of one of the most moving, even tragic, events of contemporary Indian history, the Partition."[25]

The Partition was a major political event that shattered to pieces the harmony of life and spelled disaster to millions. It ruptured many loving hearts, separated lovers, doomed countless families, uprooted innumerable people from their homes and hearths, unleashed devilish forces and exploded "the myth of the innate goodness in man" (as Khuswant Singh himself put it in an interview granted to Canadian Broadcasting Commission in 1961).

The Partition disrupted the normal course of life so much in the border region that ten million people were in flight by the summer of 1947 and about one million of them were dead by the time of the monsoon. People in the northern India were all in arms, in terror or in hiding. While bestial horrors were enacted a small village on the bank of the Sutlej with a railway spanning the river, seemed a glorious exception as it was free from communal strife. The village had only three brick buildings—the Sikh temple, the mosque and the house of the money lender Lala Ram Lal. Ram Lal's was the only Hindu family in the village. The rest of about seventy families in the village were Sikhs or Muslims, almost equal in number. Khuswant Singh shows us how the communal harmony in that village was disturbed by the forces beyond the control of the villagers and the consequences that followed. In fact, the novel illustrates the tragedy that befell several peaceful villages like Mano Majra in those days.

The novel begins with house-breaking, robbery and murder of Lala Ram Lal. Juggat Singh alias Jugga, though associated with the gang of the dacoits has not joined them in the exploit. So they throw bangles in the house of Jugga as a sign of disapproval and taunt. Jugga, released on the guarantee of good conduct and forbidden to leave the village after sunset, is lying on the sand in the riverbed at the time with his Muslim sweetheart, Nooran. Hukum Chand, the deputy commissioner of the district camping in Mano Majra, is busy in drinking and making merry with a hired prostitute Haseena. But Jugga's absence from his house that night and his inability to explain it lands him in police lock-up. There he meets a no less innocent man like Iqbal Singh, a foreign educated young man of communist leanings whose only fault is the arrival in the village at an odd time. Iqbal is humiliated and locked in the cell simply because he has aroused the suspicion of the police.

The vested interest go on spreading rumours to stoke the communal fire. Despite such provocations common people keep their head cool. Imam Baksh, the Muslim priest, cannot even dream of leaving his village for Pakistan. So he declares: "What have we to do with Pakistan? We were born here. So were our ancestors. We have lived amongst you as brothers." Meet Singh, the Sikh priest, clasps Imam Baksh, in his arms and begins to sob. So the Sikh and Muslim villagers fell into each other's arms and weep like children. They move from house to house—talking, crying, swearing love and friendship, assuring each other that it will be soon over. They are, however, naive as the socio-political forces prove too strong for them and demolish the edifice of goodwill and sanity cherished by them.

A trainload of corpses from Pakistan has already disturbed the peace of the village. Then pour in refugees crying for reprisals and hot-headed agitators. To be on the safe side, the Muslims of the village decide to go. But meanwhile, the situation deteriorates still further. As a trainload of Muslims intend to cross the bridge the next day, a plan to kill at least part of them is devised by the hot-headed. Both Jugga and Iqbal are released by the police amid this chaos, both of them are friendly to the Muslims. In case of Jugga, the concern for the Muslims becomes inseparable from his worry for Nooran, who is carrying his child. Jugga comes to know that the train carrying the Muslims is the target of the hot-headed who have stretched a rope across the first span of the bridge but a foot above the funnel of the engine to sweep off the Muslims sitting on the roof of the train. While the conspirators await the cutting of the Muslims in two, Jugga climbs the steel span of the bridge and starts slashing the rope with a small knife. He is shot dead in the process but succeeds in cutting the rope and the train carrying his beloved Nooran passes safely to Pakistan.

As to the artistic merit of the novel, we may quote Iyenger with agreement: "It could not have been an easy novel to write. The events, so recent, so terrible in their utter savagery and meaninglessness, must have defied assimilation in terms of art. Khuswant Singh, however, has succeeded through resolved limitation and rigorous selection in communicating to his readers a hint of the grossness, ghastliness and total insanity of the two-nation theory and the Partition tragedy. The pity and horror of it all!—and the novel adequately conveys them both:"[26]

> What seems most remarkable to me in the novel is the fact that its characters are not symbols of good or evil. They are neither entirely virtuous nor totally sinful. They are subject to the feelings of fear, doubt, anger and uncertainty. After the fashion of the humanists, Khuswant Singh reveals without hesitation the good that lies hidden even in anti-social elements sometimes. Thus we find that the enforcer of law and order like the sub-inspector is carried away by the prevailing mood of the public and says bluntly:

> Sometimes, Sir, one cannot restrain oneself. What do the Gandhi-caps in Delhi know about the Punjab? What is happening on the other side in Pakistan, does not matter to them. They have not lost their homes and belongings; they have not had their mothers, wives, sisters and daughters raped and murdered in the streets.[27]

Hukum Chand maintains his poise but his feelings are no better. They are revealed when he says:

> Let them get out; but be careful they do not take too much with them. Hindus from Pakistan were stripped off all their belongings before they were allowed to leave.[28]

As the situation worsens, he lapses into inactivity and maintains a pretence of responsible action only:

> Well, Inspector Sahib, let them kill. Let everyone kill. Just ask for help from other stations and keep a record of the messages you send. We must be able to prove that we did our best to stop them.[29]

Thus, the bureaucrats fail and even the elite like Iqbal prove cowards. Jugga, a 'budmash' according to his own admission, however, emerges as a triumphant power for good at the critical moment when he lays down his life to save hundreds of innocent people from massacre.

Khuswant Singh's second novel *I Shall Not Hear the Nightingale* has also some social significance. Human beings as social animals are at times confronted with a situation where personal or family interests collide with the demands of society and ethics and it is difficult for an individual to decide. *I Shall Not Hear the Nightingale* takes us to the tense days of April 1942 to April 1943 in Punjab and displays the happenings in a Sikh family. Buta Singh, the Senior Magistrate as usual has identified himself with his British masters at a time when the relations between the bureaucracy and the people are highly strained. But his son, Sher, is involved in the activities of a terrorist group of students. Sher is arrested one day and all his near and dear ones are shaken. But the young man's mother remains firm with her faith. She advises her family to have a non-stop reading of the Adi Granth for two days and two nights and to seek guidance from the Guru. While others in the family will not mind if Sher goes to the extent of securing his release by betraying his comrades, Sobhrai spends a whole night in the Gurudwara. Then she advises her son strongly against saving his skin by betraying his comrades.

The old fashioned, religious Sobhrai may not appeal to the rational mind of our age but the message that the novel conveys is likely to retain its relevance even in the times to come. And that message is: One should not betray one's comrades to save one's skin.

It may be significant to notice how even a book with such a different context can influence a younger author writing about a totally different milieu. Arundhati Roy's novel, like *Train to Pakistan* demonstrates the truth that human relations need not be limited by the barriers imposed by society. Singh's Jugga loves a Muslim woman and lays down his life to save Muslims. Heroines of Roy marry beyond their religious and ethnic group (Ammu and Rahel) and do not disapprove of such marriages in principle even after the failure of their marriages. Baby Kochamma loves an Irish Jesuit and Ammu falls in love with a Hindu Paravan. The theme of betrayal in *I Shall Not Hear the Nightingale* finds an echo in Roy's novel. The twins are tricked by Baby Kochamma into betraying the man they love so much. That shakes the twins heavily and one of them Estha loses his speech for the rest of his life.

It is not possible to discuss in detail all the earlier authors with social commitments. I try only to mention the most important figures in this tradition, and I think Shashi Deshpande deserves a discussion. It is further important to notice that she brings the topic of women's social problems into sharp focus. Her commitment consists of concentrating on the theme of meaninglessness and sexual confusion suffered by women inside a patriarchal culture. She seeks to assert thereby that the inequality of sexes is neither a biological imperative nor a divine mandate but a construct. As the principal and seminal concern of feminism is to assert the beingness of women and her novels are concerned with women's quest for self, we cannot but call her a committed feminist even though she does not feel enthusiastic about the label.[30] Women in her novels liberate themselves from external restrictions (imposed by society, culture or nature) and internal inhibitions (their own fear and guilt feelings) and establish themselves as autonomous beings. They also come to realise the fundamental truth that a person has to discover one's self oneself.

Her first novel is *The Dark Holds No Terrors* (1980). It is the story of a defiant woman Sarita (Saru for short). She develops a strong dislike for her mother who treats her son Dhruva and her daughter Sarita differently. In one of her recapitulations, Saru records her conversation with her mother:

> "Don't go out in the sun. You'll get darker."
>
> "Who cares?"
>
> "We have to care if you don't. We have to get you married."
>
> "I don't want to get married."
>
> "Will you live with us all your life?"
>
> "Why not?"
>
> "You can't."
>
> "And Dhruva?"
>
> "He is different. He is a boy."[31]

The situation worsens when her brother dies and failing to save him from drowning, she is held responsible for his death. The boy is six then and she is eleven: "You killed your brother...why didn't you die?" are the words of her mother and they drive her to show that she has every right to live.

She therefore defies her mother and goes to Bombay to study Medicine. Then she falls in love with Manohar who does not belong to her caste or class. Saru takes one more step in defiance of her mother by marrying Manohar much against her mother's wishes. Marriage, which is the promised end in a traditional society seems to Saru as the way out of her mother and her home, the first step towards autonomy. But soon she realises that marriage is no alternative to the bondage of the parental home, that her new role as a wife is no better than the role of a daughter she resented. The new situation is expressed as following:

> I had come away from my parents in a fever of excitement after the last battle. The die was cast, the decisions taken, my boats burnt. There could be no turning back. Then, this ridiculous anti-climax.[32]

While Sarita succeeds in her career of a doctor, her husband Manohar (Manu for short) grows jealous of her. Domestic discord sets in as the husband who promised to become a Shelley proves a Sadist. Now Saru becomes aware of the patriarchal view of marriage which enjoins woman to be less popular and less successful than husband:

> A wife must always be a few feet behind her husband. If he's an M.A., you should be a B.A. If he is 5′4″ tall, you shouldn't be more than tall. If he's earning Rs. 500′ you should never earn more than Rs. 499. That's only rule to follow if you want a happy marriage.[33]

Thus, she concludes that she has exchanged "one pair of pinching, torturing shoes for another," that marriage like the parental home means "the chalked lines drawn by others," that there is "no such thing between man and woman" like love and women are merely "prisoners of sex." Marriage too, like parental home appears as an enclosure. She visualizes it in terms of the dark rooms where terror awaits her.

She leaves her husband and goes to live with her father. Her mother is dead now but the escape lands her in an "atmosphere of brooding stillness" only. The neighbourhood is curious about her past and she herself feels guilty for leaving her children behind and coming to the house where her mother had died without forgiving her. So, a process of self-examination and de-construction sets in:

> The guilty sister, the undutiful daughter, the unloving wife...all persons spiked with guilts. Yes, she was all of them, she could not deny that now. She had to accept these selves to become whole again. But if she was all of them, they were not all of her. She was all these and so much more.[34]

At the end of the process she learns to free herself of guilt, shame and humiliation. She realises the mystery of human existence. In a world where human beings fail, neither her father nor her husband can be her refuge. She has to find her own way to salvation because her life is her own. She need no longer be a puppet of others. She has to look after her children and she has to attend her patients. She hates Manohar for his brutality but also pities him: "he is groping in the dark as much as I am." As everybody is lonely in the world, she need not despair. Ultimately, Sarita's fear of losing herself in the dark mysterious universe is dispelled. She becomes aware of the fact that the dark holds no terrors if you believe in your self and accept your responsibility. That gives her strength to face her 'home' and return to the profession she belongs, the proud profession of a doctor.

Her novel *Roots and Shadows* (1983) appeared later than the above but as a matter of fact, it was written first. Its theme is the identity crisis of a married woman Indu. Indu, a middle class young girl is brought up in an orthodox Brahmin family as she lost her mother at birth. The family is headed by a childless widow Akka who is the mother surrogate in the novel. Akka is a dominating woman and nothing is done in the house without her approval. Indu rebels against her and marries Jayant against her wishes. Akka believes that marriages between people of different castes and languages do not work and so she does not approve the marriage.

The marriage, however, proves disappointing. She is trapped in a loveless relationship. She loses her freedom to express her feelings and her vision becomes blurred to the extent of unclarity about her existence and her wants. Jayant condemns her to sexual repression and dishonesty by his peculiar notions and misunderstandings.

Eleven years later, Akka lies on her death-bed and calls her. Indu returns to her parental home and stays there till her death much to the surprise of her father. This 'nostros' (return home) sets in a process of re-examination of Akka and her own self that leads to her maturity and independence. Indu comes to know that Akka was not as bad as she thought. Akka's married life was traumatic and it ended when she asserted her will by forbidding her husband's concubine to see him at his death-bed. Akka's death makes her the sole inheritor of her property which establishes her identity as Akka's child. But she is reluctant to accept her as a role-model. Even Akka's house symbolises bounds of orthodoxy to her. That is why while others feel shock at the idea of demolition, she feels "both light and free." The house has been a vestige of past she wants to "move away from."

Yet, that house gives her ample opportunity to know herself. It is here she discovers her roots—an independent woman and a writer—apart from her shadows—a daughter, a mother and a commercial writer. That enables her to take firm decision about the future:

> There were other things I had to tell him (Jayant). That I was resigning my job. That I would at last do the kind of writing I had always dreamt of. That I would not, could not enrich myself with Akka's money. That, I would, on the other hand, pay for Mini's wedding.[35]

Thus she refuses to cheat herself anymore by doing things for the sake of Jayant and denying herself. She casts aside the shadows she had mistaken for her real self and asserts her own individuality. Here Deshpande seems to explode the myth of the self-denying woman and to assert the importance of self-realisation for women.

That Long Silence (1988) takes its title from a statement by Elizabeth Robins which forms the epigraph of the novel: "If I were a man and cared to know the world I lived in, I almost think it would make me a shade uneasy—the weight of the long silence of one-half of the world." The novel seeks to remove the weight by breaking the long silence that has surrounded the world of women. It traces a woman's passage through difference, guilt, fear, smothered anger and silence towards articulation and affirmation. It sums up the evolution of women through four generations the protagonist has known and looks forward to a better prospect for them.

Mohan, a middle class man indulges in some malpractices as he seeks prestige and security. Then he faces an inquiry and the possibility of losing his job. His accomplice Agarwal advises him to stay away from his office and his Churchgate flat till the dust settles. That presents no problem as the children are away on a tour with the friends of the family. So he goes to his flat at Dadar. His wife Jaya accompanies him in silent resentment. An intolerable period of anxious waiting follows which triggers off a process of self-examination and self-criticism in Jaya's mind. She is haunted and tormented by the memories of the past. She recollects her early life as well as the seventeen years of her married life. She remembers her failures and frustrations. That emotional upheaval ultimately ends giving her guidance for the future.

Mohan's crisis proves a mere storm in the tea cup and everything seems to be as it was previously in the end. But the storm that has blown over Jaya has changed her radically. She cannot remain a passive, submissive, silent housekeeper for Mohan anymore. She resolves to speak out what she has kept suppressed for seventeen years. That is necessary not for her own sake but also for the sake of other women who became victims of the male dominated society and also of their own silence. She spends two nights in putting on paper all her traumatic experiences and breaks her long silence.

Jaya's mother had to bear "the burden of pleasing others" and when that became unbearable, she lost her sanity and threw herself into a well. Then her father died early and she had to depend on her brother. Her relations conditioned her to think of marriage as her main goal in life. Jaya also discovers the waiting game early in her life because "for women the waiting game starts early in childhood. Wait until you get married. Wait until your husband comes. Wait until you go to your in-laws' home. Wait until you have kids."[36] She is taught that "a husband is like a sheltering tree" to a woman.[37] Husband becomes a "profession," a "career," a "means of livelihood" to her.[38] Then Jaya is forced to marry Mohan because her brother wants to get rid of the burden that is thrust on him.

The marriage proves no better than "a pair of bullocks yoked together."[39] She feels like a "wretch victim in bondage." There can be no question of rebelling against her husband because "a husband can do no wrong." Moreover, personal happiness is linked to social conventions by the society and it is comfortable to both to move in the same direction: "To go in different directions would be painful; and what animal would voluntarily choose pain?"[40]

The novel pinpoints how our culture keeps silent about women. At one point in the novel Jaya discovers that her name is missing in the family tree, her uncle, Ramukaka, has prepared meticulously. That is explained with the excuse that as a married woman she belongs to her husband's family. That does not satisfy her because the names of her mother, her aunts and her grandmother do not figure there either. Their names are blotted out of the family history despite all they did for the family. Thus it is a man's version of history that prevails.

Social institutions and their norms in the male-dominated society stifle the growth and free expression of the individual. They suppress normal human feelings and go to the extent of making cynics of the individuals. For example, when Jaya finds her upstairs neighbour Kamat lying dead on the floor of his flat, she leaves the place in panic and silence. Kamat, a widower and lonely man, was her best friend but she cannot pay homage to him for the fear of ruining her marriage.

Jaya's self-realization strikes a new note that deserves mention: "But what was that 'myself?' 'Trying to find oneself'—what a cliche that has become. As if there is such a thing as oneself, intact and whole, waiting to be discovered. On the contrary, there are so many, each self, attached like a Siamese twin to a self of another person, neither able to exist without the other."[41] Many people (including her mother and two grandmothers) have become part of Jaya's personality and her unconscious. That is why attempts to recall them are so much evident in the novel.

There is other discovery that is remarkable. Jaya comes to the conclusion that she has not done justice to her talents in her zeal to fulfil her roles of a wife and a mother. Years ago she wrote a story that won a first prize and was published in a magazine. That did not please Mohan because he thought the man portrayed in the story would be identified with him by the readers. Jaya continued writing under an assumed name even after that but her stories were rejected because her anger, her strong passions were censored out. As Kamat pointed out fear of writing and fear of failing were the real reasons of her failure as a writer. Rightly did he advise her: "Take yourself seriously, woman. Don't skulk behind a false name. And work-work if you want others to take you seriously."[42]

Such revelations embolden her to take hard decisions. She resolves to write fearlessly, to get off all the ghosts which have bothered her for years. She declares: "I am not afraid any more. The panic has gone. I'm Mohan's wife, I had thought and cut off the bits of me that had refused to be Mohan's wife. Now I know that kind of a fragmentation is not possible."[43]

To conclude, the heroines of Shashi Deshpande strive for self-realization and self-assertion and they succeed in it. Equality between sexes is the dream they cherish. But they seek their solutions always within the range of family. This phenomenon seems to be rooted in the very nature of feminism in India which respects the institution of family. Then, there is the psychological phenomenon called symbiosis. Eric Fromm uses this term in his book *Escape From Freedom* for the union of individuals in such a way that they lose the integrity of their self. Victimization is not only the way a victimizer controls or manipulates others, but it is also a means of controlling himself. So the victimizer needs the victim. Manohar, Jayant and Mohan need their wives desperately. As for the victim, she too needs the victimizer because it is not easy to be free. Symbiosis, thus, forms the basis of both sadism and masochism and Shashi Deshpande's novels illustrate it well. So the novels of Shashi Deshpande are significant both socially and psychologically.

Arundhati Roy shares the resentment of Shashi Deshpande about treating sons and daughters differently as evident from her observations about Chacko and Ammu in her novel. Saru in *The Dark Holds No Terrors* is blamed for the death of her brother, Ammu in Roy's novel is accused of bringing dishonour to the family and punished heavily for it. Deshpande's heroines Saru and Indu marry according to their choice, disregarding considerations like caste, class and language. We find the same spirit in Ammu and Rahel. The mother or surrogate mother is the tormentor in Deshpande's novels, father replaces her in Roy's novel. Both the novelists strongly disapprove of the practice of presenting marriage as the only goal in a woman's life. Heroines of Roy are rebels like those of Deshpande. Mammachi and Pappachi in Roy's novel illustrate the symbiotic relationship so much depicted in the novels of Deshpande discussed above.

Amarinder who belongs to medical profession deserves to be counted as a remarkable figure among the socially committed novelists. She was a gynaecologist in the prestigious All India Institute of Medical Sciences in New Delhi. Her novel *Lajo* (1990) has not received the attention and publicity it deserves. It is centred around the time of the 1984 riot that followed the murder of Mrs. Indira Gandhi by her Sikh security guards. It shows how unhealthy politics bewilders and puzzles people and triggers a crisis which it cannot control. We learn the following about the novelist's reaction to that crisis from the 'Author's Note':

> I too started my story around the time of 1984 riots and went on to narrate the repercussions this event had on the lives of thousands of Indians. A sect of people were left bewildered because they were ostracised by the majority for no other reason but for an accident of birth in a particular community.[44]

Amarinder knows from her experience how simple minds get involved in the activities of the terrorists:

> After initial numbness and shock were off there arose in their breasts emotions as varied as complete apathy to searing hatred. This set into motion a vicious circle that now seems to have no end.[45]

Amarinder wants an end of that "vicious circle" and the novel is a clarion call for the same.

The novel is divided in fourteen chapters. The last part of Chapter IV directly deals with Operation Blue Star on June 4, 1984 which leads to the murder of Indira Gandhi on October 31, 1984. To the Sikhs: "...it was Indira Gandhi who betrayed their trust in her by attacking and mutilating the sacred Golden Temple. Well, Operation Blue Star was avenged and the assassins were martyrs in the eyes of the fanatics!"[46]

Riots are the aftermath of such fanaticism. Fear strikes at the heart of every Sikh and every Sikh household feels threatened. There was a nationwide large-scale "planned genocide masterminded by politicians." Then the camp-followers and caretakers flock together to shed crocodile tears for the dead and to help the sufferers. Such meetings now so common in our sub-continent prove hypocritical as usual. As the novel puts it:

> Money donated for their welfare went into the pockets of their caretakers. Truck after truck arrived laden with food, medicines, clothing and blankets. But where did it all go? Certainly not to those for whom it was intended.[47]

Riots produce orphans and their plight is pathetic. While the rudderless, little souls with a hollow look in their eyes move about in camps, the mean-minded care-takers exploit the opportunity to make money. They demand Rs. 10,000/- for each orphan and Lajo, the heroine of the novel pays that amount to 'those people sitting in the office' to adopt an orphan called Guddi. We wonder how low people can stoop for the sake of money, how inhuman they become.

The story takes an unexpected turn in Chapters IX and X. Lajo, whose husband was killed in the riot, had assaulted an innocent person to avenge the killing of her husband in a fit of anger and taken him for dead. The victim, Vikram Kumar comes back to her alive. Lajo's reaction to his return safe and sound can be best expressed in her own words:

> ...It struck me with full force that in spite of all I loved you with all of my heart and in stabbing you I had stabbed my love and was horrified over my deed. Now I

> cannot but thank God—whichever God you or I believe in for giving you back to me.[48]

The event also brings a change in her conception of God and religion as she further declares: "Getting you back has renewed my faith in God, a universal God and yet strangely shaken my faith in the diversity of religion. Otherwise why should a Hindu God make you love me, a Sikh woman and why should I love you more than anyone else on this earth."[49]

Thus, love gives meaning, purpose and direction in life to Lajo. Love brings Lajo close to humanism but she has yet to overcome her problems. She cannot forget the cruelty and mass torture to which her kith and kin were subjected. The memory of those atrocities keeps her mind haunting and she cannot but think of revenge. Persistent ill-feelings and hatred lead her to commit the worst blunder she can. She makes Sharan a true Sikh to avenge the terrorists against her people. In other words, she prepares him for joining the Sikh terrorists unwittingly. Chapters XI and XII record the developments.

The outcome of the blunder committed by her forms the contents of Chapter XIII. Sharan, an infuriated terrorist now kills Vikram Kumar, his father. Lajo realises now that she was totally wrong in drumming communal feelings in the mind of her son. The inner conflict that sets in Lajo's mind has been well dramatised and raised to a great literary height by the novelist. Lajo repents deeply for what she has done in bitterness:

> I did everything in the name of love but then alas! that too is no excuse. Horrendous blunder I have made...I have turned son against father, because I thought it was the best thing to do at that time.[50]

Thus, we find that communalism injected in the youth poisons their minds. Anger and frustration lead them astray and culminate in violence, loot, and even murder. Politics under the circumstances becomes a weapon of prolonged social turmoil. The last chapter of the novel, 'The Ultimate Religion' seems to offer a way out. The message of the chapter is simple: humanity is "the best of all religions rather than the only religion like Sikhism, Hinduism, Islam or Christianity." In other words, we need a non-sectarian approach in individual as well as in national life. Not a false secularism but a broad, secular outlook is the remedy of the social malaise that has been tormenting our nation ever since 1947. That is what enables Lajo to admit the truth that there is actually no difference between Sharanjit Singh, a Sikh and Sharan Kumar, a Hindu:

> Because you are the same person with the same mannerism, the same nature, the same handsome face and the same faults. What matters to me is that you are a lovable human being.[51]

So, the goal of a human being ought to be to become a "lovable human being." That is the message of *Lajo* and its relevance to our times can hardly be underrated.

It is not our intention here to go into every single socially committed novel or novelist in Indo-English literature but to point out how a rich tradition does belong here and that Arundhati Roy deserves a place within this tradition. She may have been influenced to some extent by the depiction of atrocities in the name of religion in *Lajo.* Her novel is concerned about the inhuman behaviour that springs from caste prejudices, but the atrocities committed and the suffering caused are no less palpable. Syrian Christians look down upon the Hindus because of their religion but share their prejudices at the same time. They are hardly less fanatic in defending their caste prejudices than the Hindus they hate. Roy exposes their hypocrisy as vigorously as Amarinder lays bare the fanaticism of Hindu and Sikh fundamentalists in *Lajo.* She endorses the secular outlook of Amarinder in her novel and upholds the goal of 'a lovable human being.'

Thus we find that Roy's commitment has not come into being from nowhere. She has not projected some western model into Indian background. Rather, she owes a lot to her predecessors and shares many of their worries. She belongs to a tradition and tries to promote and enrich it whatever her strengths and weaknesses.

REFERENCES

1. Parameshwaran, Uma. *A Study of Representative Indo-English Novelists,* New Delhi, 1976, 16.
2. Hastings, *Encyclopedia of Religion and Ethics* (Article on Ages).

3. *Ibid.*
4. Smith, W. Robertson, *The Religion of the Semites,* London, 1927, 303 and 601.
5. Winternitz, M., *A History of Indian Literature,* English translation, Pune, 1972, Vol.I, 20 and 266.
6. Iyengar, K.R.S., *Indian Writing in English,* New Delhi, 1999, 315.
7. Walsh, William, *Indian Literature in English,* London, 1990, 63.
8. *Ibid.,* 63.
9. Sharma, K.K., (ed.), *Perspectives on Mulk Raj Anand,* Ghaziabad, 1978, 52.
10. Iyengar, *op. cit.,* 332.
11. Walsh, *op. cit.,* 63.
12. Iyengar, *op. cit.,* 335-336.
13. Walsh, *op. cit.,* 64.
14. Iyengar, *op. cit.,* 339.
15. Cowasjee, Saros, *So Many Freedoms: A Study of the Major Fiction of Mulk Raj Anand,* Madras, 1977, 53.
16. Iyengar, *op. cit.,* 340.
17. Rajan, P.K., *Mulk Raj Anand: A Revaluation,* New Delhi, 1995, 58.
18. Fisher, Merlene, *The Wisdom of the Heart: A Study of the Works of Mulk Raj Anand,* New Delhi, 1985, 38-39.
19. Iyengar, *op. cit.,* 414.
20. *Ibid.,* 416.
21. *India Today,* August 30, 1999, 55.
22. *India Today,* August 30, 1999, 54.
23. *India Today,* August 16, 1999, 75.
24. *India Today,* August 30, 1999, 52.
25. Sahane, Vasant A., *Khushwant Singh,* New York, 1972, 69.
26. Iyengar, *op. cit.,* 502.
27. Khushwant Singh, *Train to Pakistan,* Delhi, 1988, 30.
28. *Ibid.,* 32.
29. *Ibid.,* 177.
30. Deshpande, Shashi, "The Dilemma of a Woman Writer," *The Literary Criterion;* 20: 4 (1985), 33-36.
31. Deshpande, Shashi, *The Dark Holds No Terrors,* Delhi, 1980, 40.
32. *Ibid.,* 31-32.
33. *Ibid.,* 124.
34. *Ibid.,* 201.
35. Deshpande, Shashi, *Roots and Shadows,* Bombay, 1983, 205.
36. ——, *That Long Silence,* New Delhi, 1988, 30.

37. Despande, Shashi, *That Long Silence*, New Delhi, 1988, 32.
38. *Ibid.*, 75.
39. *Ibid.*, 12.
40. *Ibid.*, 12.
41. *Ibid.*, 69.
42. *Ibid.*, 148.
43. *Ibid.*, 191.
44. Amarinder, *Lajo*, Delhi, 1990, 1.
45. *Ibid.*, 1.
46. *Ibid.*, 27.
47. *Ibid.*, 44.
48. *Ibid.*, 77.
49. *Ibid.*, 77.
50. *Ibid.*, 125.
51. *Ibid.*, 133.

2

ARUNDHATI ROY: THE VOICE FOR SMALL THINGS

The earlier chapter tried to present the rich tradition of socially committed novels in English in our country, and mentioned how this thesis tries to place Arundhati Roy in that tradition. Before we proceed to examine the nature of her commitment in detail, it is befitting to introduce our readers to this author in brief.

Arundhati Roy was born in 1960 to a Syrian Christian mother and a Bengali father. The married life of her parents was a failure and they separated. This left Arundhati's mother, Mary Roy, overburdened with the responsibility of two children. Arundhati's brother Lalit is eighteen months younger than her. Mary Roy returned to her village Aymanam in the district of Kottayam in Kerala, where she lived with her children at her brother's pickle factory. The experiences at the village seem to have left a lasting impression on Arundhati. As her mother puts it: "There was much trauma for me in 1960s as Kottayam did not accept me as I was a woman separated from my husband.... It is only when I read her book that I realised that even at five she was conscious that we were unwelcome in the native home and that I expected her to be able to stand on her own feet, so that she would never be in such a weak position as I was."[1]

Mary Roy ran an informal school called Corpus Christi at Aymanam which imparted western-based education to the elite of the area. Arundhati spent her formative years there and acquired her literary and intellectual abilities. That she discovered the joy of reading there, seems to have contributed a lot to the development of her personality. Quite remarkable is her mother's observation about her education: "She joined a formal school only at eleven. I believe one learns much more in the absence of a vigorous syllabus."[2]

Arundhati's abilities seem to have become evident early in her life. Her mother remarks: "Arundhati is a born talker and a born writer. While she was studying in our school it was a problem to find a teacher who could cope with her voracious appetite for reading and writing. Most of the time she educated herself. I can remember our vice-principal Sneha Zakaria resorting to Shakespeare's *Tempest* as a text for this little fourth-grader."[3]

Despite difficulties, Arundhati continued her education. She left Kerala at the age of eighteen and studied architecture at Delhi. She got a scholarship and went to Italy. Then, she spent some time at Goa coast selling shirts made of Benarasi Saris. Soon, she returned to Delhi and rented a 'barsati' near Nizamuddin Dargah and hired a cycle at the rate of Rupees two per day. She worked at the National Institute of Urban Affairs at the time. Pradip Krishen saw her coming from the opposite direction one day during the period and selected her for acting as a tribal girl in his film 'Massey Saheb.' Though she was reluctant at first, she complied with the request subsequently. She wrote scripts for Pradip Krishen's films 'In Which Annie Gives It Those Ones' and 'Electric Moon.' The first one got a National Award. She wrote screenplay for the T. V. serial 'The Banyan Tree' also. The contact and collaboration with Pradip Krishen culminated in her marriage with this film director.[4]

One of the happy moments in her life was a gift from her mother of "Baby Remington Typewriter"—"Just the right thing for a writer" (as Arundhati reacted). Soon she exchanged it for a desk-top computer, and wrote her novel *The God of Small Things* on it. She wrote it quietly and took four years to complete it. The novel was completed on April 6, 1996. She told Vir Sanghvi, the editor of *Sunday*: "I just started putting down what was going on my head.... It was all just coming out of me, like smoke I suppose, and I kept putting it down."[5]

The events took a dramatic turn after the manuscript was ready in 1997. "Pankaj Mishra, the local agent of Harper

Collins in India, appeared, as if from nowhere, in the middle of night to call up Arundhati Roy to convey the news that the book was 'astoundingly good.' Within four days, the British literary agent, David Goodwin, landed up at her door with a hefty advance. This happened in the middle of May. By the end of June, the book was sold to eighteen countries for over one million dollars."[6]

Arundhati Roy and her publishers took meticulous care about the typeset, cover design and other details of the quality and production and the publicity the book received was undoubtedly the result of a well-planned strategy, a fact so much emphasized by her detractors.

She won the Booker Prize for the novel in mid-October 1997. The news got enthusiastic coverage in the media. The Booker Prize for fiction set up in 1968 carries an award of 20,000 pound sterling for the best writing of the year and the authors of the Commonwealth countries only are eligible for it. Four books with Indian names or by writers of Indian origin had won the prize before Arundhati Roy, namely, V.S. Naipaul's *In a Free State* (1972), I.G. Farrel's *The Siege of Krishnapur* (1973), Ruth Prawer Jhabwala's *Heat and Dust* (1975), Salman Rushdie's *Midnight's Children* (1981). But the writers were either non-citizens or non-resident Indians. So Arundhati Roy is often said to be the first Indian to win the Booker.

The rules for the Booker Prize were modified in 1997 to limit the entries. Still, eighty-eight titles were officially submitted and the judges called in eighteen more in addition to that. Then, the books were shortlisted and six novels remained there for consideration including *Grace Notes* by Belfast-born Bernard Maclaverty, *Quarantine* by Jim Grace, *Europa* by Tim Parks, *Underground Man* by Mick Jackson and *The Essence of the Thing* by Kadeleine St. John. Arundhati Roy and Mick Jackson were the two first time novelists in the contest. Finally, the judges decided in favour of Arundhati Roy and their decision was unanimous.

The book has been translated in thirty-eight languages, though not in Indian languages. President K.R. Narayanan congratulated her on getting the Booker and added: "I feel particularly proud as you hail from my own district of Kottayam." Alice Truax wrote in *The New York Times Book Review* that "the quality of Ms. Roy's narration is so extraordinary—at once so morally strenuous and so imaginatively supple—that the reader remains enthralled all the way through to its agonizing finish." Susan Douglas, another journalist, found its reading "like eating a chocolate bomb—you take small bites and slowly savor the layers.... The book is about the gorgeousness of language." Tom Hiney observed: "One can only strongly recommend this extremely funny and enchanting and pretty much genius piece of debut fiction." The American novelist Amanda Craig opined that *The God of Small Things* is "not just this year's India novel. Nor is it, as publishers unwisely claim, a masterpiece. It is, however, written by someone who shows every promise of being capable of producing such a thing in the future."

M. Krishnan Nair, an eminent literary critic, remarked: "Roy has universalized Ayemenem, like Gabriel G. Marquez's Mocondo and R.K. Narayan's Malgudi." O.V. Vijayan wrote: "There is an innocence about Roy's book, a lack of parading." Amitav Ghosh declared: "This is the best thing that could have happened in the 50th year." Anita Desai praised Arundhati Roy and observed: "When we wrote, we tended to write based on the literature we read, not on the way people spoke. I congratulate Arundhati Roy. The new writers have made this language legitimate." Kamala Das remarked: "We didn't take English lightly.... But Arundhati Roy uses English as plaything. She can spit at correct English. She is Cinderella and fame is her prince." She further added: "She is lucky. We are not. But she is our child and we are very happy for her. Because she is young to enjoy it."

There has been much adverse criticism of *The God of Small Things* as well. Ranjana Ash did not like the praise the novel had received: "The British public always thinks that the one who makes the most money has something special. I haven't read Roy's book except in extracts. I wasn't impressed." Manjula Padmanabhan observed in the same vein: "No serious writer can believe in hype; it might sell books but it can't make a book into great literature." C.D. Narasimhaih compared her success to the "success of circus show"—and found Booker

Prize "worth no more than baker's burnt bread." C. Sathyamala revealed that language innovations in Arundhati Roy's work were done fifty years ago by Enid Blyton and *The God of Small Things* was no better than an imitation of Toni Morrison's *Beloved.*[7] To Shobha De its success appeared to be "a freak thing." Khuswant Singh observed: "Moneywise she has achieved more than anyone else."

The novel was criticised by the CPI(M) intellectuals as "anti-communist" for its references to E.M.S. Namboodripad and for presenting the Kerala communists in a far from appreciative way. So Aizaz Ahmad declared that Arundhati Roy has "neither a feel for communist politics nor perhaps rudimentary knowledge of it."[8] Christian orthodoxy joined the protest with them. Abu Abraham remarked: "Respectable Syrian Christians must feel that the book maligns the community and particularly its womanhood. The explicit references to sex are bad enough, but that a Syrian Christian woman would make love to an untouchable youth is clearly obscene."[9] Criticism of the type has not remained confined to speeches and articles, it has been carried to court. A case against Arundhati Roy was filed under section 292 of the IPC for charges of obscenity in a Kerala court which remains unresolved to date. That is perhaps the reason that the novel has not as yet been translated in Indian languages. There were proposals for making a film based on the novel but Arundhati Roy has brushed them aside because she thinks that her novel is not filmable.

Though *The God of Small Things* remains Arundhati Roy's only contribution to literature to date, her bio-data will remain incomplete if we fail to mention her writings on matters of social importance. The first one of these *The End of Imagination* was published in an English weekly *The Outlook* on August 3, 1998, 62-71. Later it appeared as a pamphlet from Kottayam in October, 1998 published by D.C. Books for 'The Campaign Against Nuclear Weapons in India.' It is a pithy argument against the nuclear weapons programme of the Indian government. Needless to say, it appears to be opposed to the general mood of the people who regard it as a matter of national pride.

The other book by Arundhati Roy, *The Greater Common Good* was published by India Book Distributors, Bombay in 1999. The royalties for the Book are assigned to the Narmada Bachao Andolan, a cause she has identified herself with. The book pleads against the construction of big dams which cause immense human suffering by depriving people of their home as well as their means of livelihood and destroy beyond recovery valuable flora and fauna. Thus both of her booklets reveal a concern for both human beings and their environment.

As a person she is warm and outgoing. Her novel describes one of its characters as follows: "She was in jeans and white T-shirt.... A tiny diamond gleaned in one nostril. She had absolutely beautiful collar bones...."[10] This statement about Rahel applies to the author as well. She is generally clad in jeans and T-shirt," though wears saris occasionally. As her mother Mary Roy remarked, she is a born talker and as such she likes to meet people. The "acknowledgements" of the novel names more than a dozen people "for seeing me through the years it took me to write this book."

Critics have discussed a lot about the imagery of Arundhati Roy.[11] A glance at the discussion reveals that Arundhati Roy is a person endowed with keen senses which enables her to distinguish between different shades of colours, varying types of smell and numerous kinds of sound. A laborious study of her similes and metaphors is required to ascertain how far she is indebted to literary sources for them, but part of them appear to be quite original to me. Though we cannot identify her totally with her creation, Rahel, she seems to share some of her traits like non-conformity to conventions, curiosity and playfulness. Playfulness often leads children to splitting words into two or three parts, using capital letters arbitrarily and reading or writing backwards. But as children grow up, they forget such fun. Arundhati Roy has retained this playfulness even after crossing thirty. And that is the secret behind her innovations in language. The same playfulness has suggested to her the idea of living one's life backwards and created the strange character of Baby Kochamma. I have been careful in drawing conclusions about her from her novel because her brother L.K.C. Roy, in an interview, spoke of her flair for adding spice to her stories[12] and the little I have drawn, I hope, will not be disputed.

Herself born of a Bengali Hindu father and a Kerala's Syrian Christian mother, Arundhati is married to Pradip Krishen, a man from Hindi-speaking region. She has got two daughters Pia and Mithva. Their names indicate how much she has got integrated to the milieu around her. Thus, she has become an embodiment of secularism and national integration in an epoch disturbed with the rise of religious fanaticism and regional sectarianism.

Arundhati Roy takes her involvement with the life around her a stage further. Social commitment is almost a trait of her personality. The very title of the novel, *The God of Small Things* implies the nature of her commitment. But before recording the same, it is desirable to see what critics think about the title—its origin, propriety and implications.

Shashibala Talwar and R.S. Sharma trace the origin of the title to Salman Rushdie's *Midnight's Children*. Saleem, the hero of that novel is worried about a slight error in specifying a certain date. Padma, his beloved, remarks under the circumstances: "What are you so long for in your face? Everybody forgets some small things, all the time." That raises a question in the mind of Saleem: "But if small things go, will large things be close behind?"[13]

C. Sathyamala detects "more than a passing resemblance" between *The God of Small Things* and Toni Morrison's *Beloved*. The theme as well as some of the expressions are similar in the two books. Sathyamala suggests that even the title bears the imprint of Toni Morrison because Paul D. reminisces in the *Beloved*: "So you protected yourself and loved small. Picked the tiniest stars out of the sky to own...."[14]

Urbashi Barat finds in the title an indication of "its moorings in myth. *The God of Small Things* is clearly related to what sociologists and cultural anthropologists in India today refer to as the Little Gods of the Hindu tradition, the deities of folklore and of everyday worship, as contrasted with the deities of the Great Tradition, imposing, autocratic, awe-inspiring."[15] She goes on to add: "*The God of Small Things* can at best bring about resilience and indifference to suffering, but Big

God is manifested in the evil of Pappachi and Baby Kochamma, the hypocrisy of Mammachi and Comrade Pillai, the anger of Chacko and Margaret Kochamma, the sense of superiority in Sophie Mol, the sodomizing Orangedrink Lemondrink Man."[16]

There can be no gainsaying the fact that Arundhati Roy had read Rushdie and Morrison before she wrote the novel and the reading might have suggested the title. As for Urbashi Barat, she has made her point well in her essay. But her emphasis is on the first part of the title, that is, 'god,' while there is much in the novel to show that Arundhati Roy's main concern is about "small things," small things that combine to make up the texture of our lives.

On page 3 of the novel, the author refers to Estha's experiences at Abhilash Talkies and the tomato sandwitches he ate on the Madras Mail and concludes: "And these are only the small things."

During the funeral of Sophie Mol, "she (Mammachi) looked small and ill in her crisp off-white Sari," we learn on page 5.

On page 19, Rahel is described as "something still and small."

We find two oft-quoted paragraphs about the Big God and Small God on the same page.

The very title of Chapter III is 'Big Man the Laltain, Small Man the Mombatti' and an explanation of the same appears on page 89.

On page 173, Margaret and her daughter are welcomed at the house of Chacko: "And once again, only the Small Things were said. The Big Things lurked unsaid inside."

On page 181 both 'small' and 'big' are mentioned: "As she grew older, Ammu learned to live with this cold, calculating cruelty. She developed a lofty sense of injustice and the mulish, reckless streak that develops in Someone Small who has been bullied all their lives by Someone Big."

Chapter XI of the novel is entitled, *The God of Small Things*. Ammu has a dream here and she wonders: "Who was he, the one-armed man? Who *could* he have been? The God of Loss? The God of Small Things? The God of Goose Bumps and Sudden Smiles? Of sour metal smells-like steel bus-rails and the smell of the bus conductor's hands from holding them?" (217).

On page 220, we find: "She knew who he was—the God of Loss, the God of Small Things. Of course she did."

On page 224, we read: "So if she were granted one small wish perhaps it would only have been Not to Know." And on the same page we notice the following: "Hooded in her own hair, Ammu leaned against herself in the bathroom mirror and tried to weep.

For herself.

For the God of Small Things."

One page 265 we find: "Perhaps this was because she (Margaret Kochamma) never really knew him, nor ever heard what hapened to him. The God of Loss. The God of Small Things."

On page 290 we read: "He was walking swiftly now, towards the Heart of Darkness. As lonely as a wolf.

The God of Loss.

The God of Small Things."

On page 330, we find again a reference to Ammu's dream:

Who was he?

Who could he have been?

The God of Loss.

The God of Small Things.

The God of Goose Bumps and Sudden Smiles.

On page 338 we read: "Even later, on the thirteen nights that followed this one, instinctively they stuck to the Small Things. The Big Things ever lurked inside. They knew that there was nowhere for them to go. They had nothing. No future. So they stuck to the small things."

It is claimed by Arundhati Roy that she was not sure of the title till she finished the book, "The novel did not have a title until the very last minute. I didn't know what to call it, there were lots of ideas and suggestions but I remember printing out the manuscript and just printing out the title at the last minute." She goes on to add: "One of the chapters was called 'The God of Small Things.' I don't know how it happened...when I read the book now I can't believe the amount of references there are to small things, but it was absolutely not the case that I started with the title and built the novel around it."[17]

We need not dispute the statement of the author about the title but that does not belie our idea of her concern. In one of the interviews granted to the press, she is reported to have said: "Fiction for me has been a way of trying to make sense of the world as I know it.... If I had to put it very simply, it is about trying to make the connections between the very smallest things and the very biggest things and to see how those fit together."[18]

Shashibala Talwar and R.S. Sharma have concluded from the author's own explanation that *The God of Small Things* "stands for the life of the weak and the helpless, whether they are small creatures like blue bottles, frogs and ants or human beings such as the victims of Hollick's lust or the women who supply Chacko's 'man's needs' or children like Estha and Rahel.... *The God of Small Things* represents all those people who are victimized by the forces of history, dead convention, false pride and respectability, the tyranny of the state and the politics of opportunism and andro-centric order."[19]

Though the text is not explicit about it, a careful reader will not fail to make out what Arundhali Roy means. All that leads to power, prestige and wealth is widely held as 'big' while the rest is relegated to the position of 'small things.' But all that is deemed as inconsequential is not necessarily so. There are many things that do not lead to power, prestige or wealth, but satisfy basic needs of human body and mind. There are also things that cannot be ignored by those who care for the well-being of the living beings in general. The narrow-minded persons who care for personal interests only are generally inclined to disregard such "small things."

But "small things" need not refer to inanimate objects only. There is no lack of selfish, cruel people in our society who treat the poor and the powerless no better than "small things." They reduce beings or persons to objects which can be broken, crushed, thrown away or destroyed at the sweet will of the powerful. Their fate, nay even their life, is immaterial to those who wield power. They are unable to raise their voice against the injustice done to them. As they are voiceless, as they cannot resist, they are but "small things."

We are now in a position to conclude that Arundhati Roy has a deep concern for the "small things" and her commitment is related to them. We have seen what the "small things" mean. They are the victims of state, society and sheer will of the unthinking powerful. Though the term "small things" implies a lot and defies an exhaustive enumeration and elaboration, we can broadly put it in the following four categories:

Women who are placed in a subordinate position by society and left defenceless by the state.

Children who are unable to defend themselves and suffer a lot to survive.

The workers and the *dalits* who are downtrodden, exploited and abused traditionally.

The environment which is subjected to wanton acts of manipulation and destruction. They are the voiceless Arundhati Roy has raised her voice for.

Her commitment issues from her worldview and we have to consider her novel in the light of the rest of her literary and social activities. She argues in an interview: "As far as I am concerned, whether the protest is about Nuclear Weapons or Big Dams on the Narmada, what one is fighting for is nothing less than a worldview, a way of seeing. Why, even *The God of Small Things* is a worldview. What all of these works have in common is that they attempt to analyse power and powerlessness."[20]

Thus, having outlined the nature of the novelist, we proceed to analyse her treatment of the four categories of the "small" in the following chapters.

REFERENCES

1. Mary Roy quoted in *The Critical Studies of Arundhati Roy's The God of Small Things* edited by Joydip Singh Dodiya and Jaya Chakraborty, New Delhi, 1999, 5-6.
2. Dhawan, R.K., (ed), *Arundhati Roy The Novelist Extraordinary*, New Delhi, 1999, 14.

3. Dodiya and Chakraborty, *op. cit.*, 5.
4. *Desh* (Bengali Fortnightly), June 14, 1997, 102-104.
5. Dhawan, *op. cit.*, 16.
6. *Ibid.*, 16.
7. Dhawan, *op. cit.*, 15, 25, 32-34, 385-396; and Dodiya and Chakraborty, *op. cit.*, 4-5
8. Ahmad, A., 'Reading Arundhati Roy Politically,' *Frontline*, August 8, 1997, 103-108.
9. Abraham, Abu, 'Breaking the Love Laws,' *The Hindustan Times Sunday Magazine*, November 23, 1997, 3.
10. Roy, Arundhati, *The God of Small Things*, London, 1998, 18 [All references to the novel will be made to this edition only].
11. Sharma, R.S., and Talwar, Shashibala, *Arundhati Roy's The God of Small Things: Critique and Commentary*, New Delhi, 1998, 84-95; Bhatt, Indira and Nityanandam, Indira (ed.), *Explorations: Arundhati Roy's The God of Small Things*, New Delhi, 1999, 130-135.
12. Kumar, C. Sujitchandra, 'Facts and Fiction,' *The Week*, Vol. 15, No. 45 (Oct. 26, 1997), 43.
13. Sharma and Talwar, *op. cit*, 199.
14. Dhawan, *op. cit.*, 395.
15. Bhatt and Nityanandam, *op. cit.*, 71.
16. *Ibid.*, 73.
17. Dhawan, *op. cit.*, 19-20.
18. *General Knowledge Today* Nov. 1997, 6.
19. Sharma and Talwar, *op. cit.*, 43.
20. *Frontline*, Aug. 27, 1999, 132.

3

THE WOMEN IN THE NOVEL

One of the categories of "small things" Arundhati Roy cares for consists of women. There can be no gainsaying that despite all the socio-economic developments during the last two centuries, women do not occupy an enviable position in society. It is relevant, therefore, to look into the causes that have kept them in subordination and relegated them to the status of the second sex.

"The laws of ancient India were so catholic in spirit and all-embracing; if they are taken in their true spirit, they can cover the entire needs of humanity. At the time when these laws were framed, no country in the world produced better laws for womanhood, nor gave a higher status to women in society." That is how Shakuntala Rao Shastri concludes her survey of the sacred laws of India.[1] As a Sanskrit scholar, she is expected to know better than others and perhaps she is right. But the trouble with the sacred laws is that their "spirit" is grasped differently by people according to their position in society and their interests. Moreover, Indian society is governed more by tradition (which includes customs, superstitions, prejudices as well as religious injunctions) than by sacred laws. It is not unusual to find that people continue to pay lip service to the sacred text but depart from its laws in practice for various reasons. Therefore, it is necessary to reckon with the tradition instead of invoking the spirit of the sacred laws.

Indian society has practised an extreme form of patriarchy since the beginning of known history, though the relics of matriarchy were found as late as the nineteenth century in certain regions. It is based on male predominance and female subordination. It praises the wife-mother role of women but treats her as no better than the legal, economic and sexual property of her husband. This is sanctified by socio-legal treatises. Thus it is laid down in the Laws of Manu that "No act is to be done according to her own will by a young girl, a young woman, though she be in her own house. In her childhood a girl should be under the will of her father; in her youth under that of her husband; her husband being dead, under the will of her sons. A woman should never enjoy her own will. Though of bad conduct or debauched, a husband must always be worshipped like a god by a good wife."[2]

Woman began her course of life as a member of an extended family which was a small community in itself as it spanned several generations and comprised of the patriarch and his younger brothers with their families, married sons and their families, all the unmarried sons and daughters, and widowed or deserted daughters who returned to their parental home. There were gradations based on sex, age and degree of relationship with the head of the family. All the males born in the family inherited the ancestral wealth but the daughters were not entitled to a share. They were compensated at marriage with jewellery, clothes and household articles which was originally intended to be "woman's wealth" solely under their control. Eventually, however, it became transmuted into "dowry" which was demanded by husband and marital family. Thus women lost all their assets in course of time and became economically dependent.

Elders, even parents, did not treat male and female children equally. The family betrayed a strong pro-son bias because the son would remain in the family, carry on the family name, care for parents in old age and perform the necessary rituals after their death. The daughter was viewed as "stranger's wealth" because she was to be given away in marriage at a great expense as dowry had to be paid for the purpose. So a woman counted less in family and a low premium was placed on her life.

This set-up led to violence against woman almost as soon as she was born and female infanticide was prevalent in certain regions of the country. It was forbidden by law in 1877 but the woman remained unwelcome and undesirable.

A daughter could not have a carefree childhood because she had to handle household duties and undergo chastisement as a preparation for married life. Education was denied to her even among the traditionally literate upper classes who deemed education a must for boys.

The girls were married well before puberty and sent to their husband's house as soon as they came of age. A strong bond between wives and husbands could not develop under the extended family. Nor could there develop a female bond among the unrelated outsiders who came in as daughters-in-laws. They were all dependent persons competing for a better share in the resources of the family.

With the early start of married life came the early motherhood which was physically traumatic, debilitating and injurious upto the point of death. If the wife failed to produce a child or bore female children only, she was treated as an offender of the worst kind. That could be an excuse for her being deserted by her husband. If she was not deserted, her husband would marry again and have an additional wife to ensure a male heir. Ignorant of the elementary facts of genetics, people laid the blame for barrenness or birth of female children on the wife only.

If the husband died earlier, the wife had to undergo a lot of traumatic experiences. In some parts of India, like Bengal and Rajasthan, widows were immolated on the funeral pyre of their husband. The practice was legally stopped in 1829. In the regions which did not practise widow immolation, they had to live on sufferance. They had to wear drab clothes and to renounce all sort of pleasure. Sometimes they were physically disfigured, for example, by shaving off their heads. They were deemed inauspicious and kept away from all ceremonies in the family except, of course, mourning. There were strict rules for their food. The widows, along with the deserted women, were treated as household drudges. Though widowers could and did remarry, the widows could not in case of upper castes. It must be mentioned that most of those widows lost their husband early in childhood as marriage took place early and difference in age between wife and husband was quite appalling upto the nineteenth century, which made widowhood inevitable. The Widow Remarriage Act of 1856 legalised remarriage of the widows but that brought little change in reality.

Tradition was challenged by various factors that came along with the contact with the west. One of these challenges came from the Christian missionaries. Initially they were zealous critics of Hinduism and missed no opportunity to find fault with the scriptures and social conduct of the Hindus. Then, the introduction of the western type of education in India left the door open for new ideas. First came the ideas of Mill, Spencer, Bentham, Thomas Paine and Voltaire and then those of Mazini, Garibaldi, Kamal Pasha etc. and finally Marxism.

Initially the attitude of the elite in India was defensive, a trend which continues to date. Weaknesses of the social practices were admitted without much ado, but it was pointed out that they issued not from the scriptures but from a departure from the same. Rammohun Roy based himself on the scriptures while propagating against the immolation of the widows and Vidyasagar argued for the remarriage of the widows in the same fashion. They sought reforms but proceeded with due regard to their own patriotic feelings and nostalgia as well of the country men. Also, they must have felt that this was the best tactic to follow in order to influence their orthodox countrymen. Part of the elite felt bold enough to think and express freely much later and gradually, about the second decade of the twentieth century.

Demands for social reform were conceded from time to time. Immolation of the widows was banned legally in 1829 and remarriage of the widows was—legalised in 1856 thanks to the efforts of Raja Rammohun Roy and Vidyasagar respectively. Then came legislation prohibiting child marriages and giving more rights to women in respect of marriage, divorce, inheritance etc. Such measures met a lot of resistance from religious bigots. In case of the religious minorities the progress has been much slow for the same reasons. Impact of the legislation as well as of western ideas has not been even in different regions and classes.

Women played a significant role in the socio-political life of the country in the new age. As early as 1880s, Madam

Cama (a Parsi woman from Bombay) figures in the world socialist movement. Sarojini Naidu, Kamaladevi Chattopadhyaya, Aruna Asafali, Sucheta Kripalani and several others rose to leading positions in the national movement. Women fought against the British, gun in hands, first as members of the secret organisations like Anushilan Samiti and Jugantar and then in the ranks of INA. It is quite natural, therefore, that nobody questioned their franchise in India. They got not only voting rights before their sisters in Switzerland, they got positions like ministers, governors and ambassadors well before several western countries could grant the same to women. India had a woman prime minister too for a period of over two decades.

But despite all that, we have little reason to be complacent about the condition of women in India. While the universal demographic pattern shows a female surplus, the sex ratio in India reveals a female deficit. The general proportion of women in the total population is not only unbalanced but also declining consistently. The census of 1901 showed 972 females per 1000 males, in 1991 it dropped to 929 females per 1000 males. The demographers explain it as a result of frequently inadequate nutrition and healthcare which causes higher mortality among women.

That is, however, a passive form of violence to women. But other forms of violence have not disappeared despite modernisation. Mostly, they are practised in other decisive ways. Formerly, female infanticide was very common in certain regions of the country. In the Bhatti community of Jaisalmer (Rajasthan) the sex ratio is 550 women to 1000 men only as against the national ratio of 929 to 1000. Marriage parties have not visited the villages of the community for decades. It was reported in 1988 by Rajendra Singh, a member of the community, that forty girls were murdered soon after their birth in the community.

But the urban, educated and relatively well-off people are employing sophisticated means instead of the crude ones. Diagnostic technique of amniocentesis, basically designed for detecting foetal abnormalities, is harnessed to determine the sex of the foetus and followed by selective abortion of female foetuses. Only two states in India, namely Maharashtra and Goa, have attempted to stop it by legislation.

The Constitution of India provides for compulsory education for all upto the age of fourteen, but this is generally neglected in case of girls. The percentage of girls attending school varies from state to state, sometimes it is below 20% and rarely reaches 50%. Female literacy in India is 24.8% as compared to the male literacy of 46.9%. This deplorable state keeps women ignorant of their rights and unable to exercise them.

Though the educated young people in upper middle and upper classes are asserting their choice to some extent, most of the marriages are still arranged by the families of the bride and groom. Though the Child Marriage Restraint Act passed in the early part of the twentieth century forbids it, infants are still married in certain states like Rajasthan. It is estimated that fourteen million child marriages take place in India every year. The mean age for marriage in India is 23.3 for men and 18.3 years for women. However, regional variations are glaring with 21.8 years for women in Kerala and 16.1 years in Rajasthan. In Uttar Pradesh, Madhya Pradesh, Bihar and Rajasthan, 50% of the girls are married before the age of sixteen. Early marriage, frequent pregnancies and deliveries take their toll and complications in child birth cause 13% of the deaths before the twenty-fifth year.

Maternal mortality in India is 500 per 100,000 live births. The danger of death is greatest when the mother is below twenty-five years and above thirty-five years. The average Indian woman becomes pregnant eight times, gives birth to six to seven children out of which four survive. Eight per cent of a woman's reproductive life seems to be spent in pregnancy and lactation.

The entire process of arranging the marriage is humiliating to women. A girl has to show her skills and undergo a long test and interrogation by parents and guardians of the potential groom. The boy is rarely asked a question or required to prove his abilities. The traumatic experience is worsened when the girl is rejected for some reason or other and has to confront interrogation teams before selection. Even then the question of dowry remains. The girls who do not have parents or guardians to arrange and pay a dowry hardly get married. Educated people are allowing some freedom to their daughters and delaying their marriages but considerations of caste, community and religion are rarely brushed aside even there.

Demands for dowry before and after marriage do not seem to have diminished by legislation and education. Women are harassed and tortured for extorting more money and consumer goods which results sometimes in death (either through suicide or outright murder). Often such deaths are camouflaged as accidents, if not suicide due to mental derangement. Despite the Dowry Prohibition Act of 1986, the number of dowry deaths increased from 1912 in 1987 to 5154 in 1991 and cases of cruelty by the husband and his relatives have increased from 11603 in 1989 to 15949 in 1991.[3] The culprits even if arrested are rarely punished. The practice of wife-battering remains though it varies in degree from region to region and class to class. However, such cases are seldom reported to the police.

Daughters are still treated as outsiders. Once married they are welcome in the parental home on limited occasions only. They are reminded again and again: "Your place is next to your husband. Your home is where he is." So when they are abused and forced to flee, they rarely find a sympathetic response at the parental home. Attempts at "reconciliation" are made ignoring the gravity of situation which often leads to an untimely end of their lives. Divorced or separated women are deemed an unnecessary burden to the parental home and somewhat guilty rather than victims by the society. Responsibility for the failure of marriage is generally laid at the door of wife ignoring the truth that the husband, the in-laws too play a role.

The Hindu Succession Bill of 1955-56 entitles Hindu daughters equal rights of inheritance in their father's estate. But property rights to wives are denied by religious or personal laws. Divorced wives enjoy no rights to the husband's property. Wives have the "right to reside" in their matrimonial homes only during the pendency of marriage.

Economic constraints have necessitated middle class women to seek jobs to supplement the family income. But their choice is generally limited to nursing, teaching etc. which are deemed suitable for women. Employment, however, does not give them control over their income. They are expected to hand over their salary to their husband or in-laws and keep contented with the petty amounts granted to them for their daily expenses. Their lives are further complicated by the problems of managing both the job and the home, alcoholic husbands squandering away their earnings and the suspicions about their character.

Lower class women have been always working. Though the principle of "equal wages for equal work" is never challenged, women are paid less than men for the same work. The other problem they face frequently is sexual harassment and abuse. In a country where a senior minister dares molest an air-hostess, one can imagine the lot of the lower class women.

According to the figures and records of the National Crime Bureau submitted in Parliament, a rape case occurs in India every 54 minutes and harassment to a woman every 34 minutes. In 1987 the reported cases of harassment were 16292 which rose to 20611 in 1991 (an increase of 26.5%) while rape figures rose from 7767 to 9738 during the same period (an increase of 26.1%).[4] There were about one hundred cases of rape annually reported by women belonging to scheduled castes and tribes in late '80s according to official records. Most of them were committed by security forces. A law promulgated in September 1989 sought to protect the vulnerable section but rape by police and paramilitary forces remains wide-spread. Often it is "well-planned and premeditated" sexual assault on women like the gang rape of twenty women in Pararia village in Bihar in 1988 shown in the documentary film "Rape as Assertion of Power" directed by Sagari Chhabra. As the village was the first to be submerged under water due to a major dam project, the villagers were demanding adequate compensation for their land. The gang rape was designed to quell the protest.[5]

Such atrocities are not confined to some backward regions only. Even from the village Thirunelli in Kerala three hundred unmarried tribal women were reported to have become mothers and they were all victims of rape by non-tribal people.

Criminals generally go unpunished by the courts on technical grounds if they happen to be rich and powerful. A case to the point is that of Santosh Singh, the son of a serving IGP who raped and killed the twenty four year old Delhi University student Priyadarshini Mattoo in January, 1996.[6]

In case of the poor and illiterate victims a class bias is often evident. The women of lower classes are supposed to have nothing like character and so charges of molestation and rape are dismissed lightly if they happen to be the victims. Often, they are alleged to be lying in order to extort some money and that is the excuse for setting at liberty the accused belonging to upper classes by the judges.

An important development during the last three decades has been the appearance of some women's journals which have departed from the practice of discussing food, fashion and cinema and devoted themselves to the real problems of women. Along with them, a number of women's organisations have come into being. Thus an organised movement to raise the consciousness of women has started. Resistance to harassment, cruelty and discrimination against women is no longer sporadic or isolated. It is finding an organised expression and emboldening women to assert their rights. Reservation of thirty per cent of seats for women at the panchayet level is also bringing a change for better in the villages where the majority of our country lives. It will make more and more difficult to ignore, hoodwink or suppress women.

The God of Small Things is a product of the social reality described above. The events of the novel take place in Kerala and women characters of it are without exception, Syrian Christians. As they are a religious group separate from the Hindus, what applies to the majority of the country may not be expected to apply to them too. So a few words about the Syrian Christians become relevant and even necessary.

As Krishna Chaitanya puts it in his book *Kerala*, Christianity is believed to have come to Kerala three centuries before it gained recognition in Europe and became the established religion of Rome. St. Thomas the Apostle reached Kerala and founded several churches along the coast according to the tradition. Pantaenus of Alexandria found a flourishing Christian community in the second century. And then came an influx of Syrian immigrants of four hundred Christians from seventy two families of Baghdad, Nineveh and Jerusalem led by the merchant, Thomas of Cana. The community played a significant role in the economic life of Kerala and received the patronisation of its rulers—a fact well documented by inscriptions.

The Portuguese struck a note of discord and attempted to thwart the integration of the Christians in Kerala's socio-cultural life. The Portuguese who belonged to the Roman Catholic Church attempted to bring all the Apostolic Christian Community under their fold and to Latinise their rites. The attempt failed as the community refused to recognise the Jesuit priests as spiritual heads. Thus a separate evolution of the Jacobite (Syrian) Church was finally affirmed and assured in 1623.[7]

The crude, ruthless methods the Jesuits used in their endeavour to establish their supremacy is indicated well by Arundhati Roy when she writes (besides other things): "Before three purple-robed Syrian Bishops murdered by the Portuguese were found floating in the sea, with coiled sea serpents riding on their chests and oysters in their tangled beards."[8]

Arundhati Roy furnishes another piece of information which is relevant to understand her characters: "Twenty per cent of Kerala's population were Syrian Christians, who believed that they were descendants of one hundred Brahmins whom Saint Thomas the Apostle converted to Christianity when he travelled east after Resurrection."[9] With the pride of this ancestry go all the prejudices about caste and all the bias that berate women.

Even Kochu Maria, the cook shares such prejudices. We find the following about her: "...Her kunukku earrings were thick and gold.... Kochu Maria couldn't stop wearing her kunukku because if she did, how could people know that despite her petty cook's job (seventy five rupees a month) she was a Syrian Christian, Mar Thomite? Not a Pelaya, or a Pulaya, or a Paravan. But a touchable, upper-caste Christian (into whom Christianity had seeped like tea from a teabag)."[10]

There are two references to inbreeding among Syrian Christians. First, "Chacko said that Estha and Rahel were indecently healthy. And so was Sophie Mol. He said that it was because they didn't suffer from inbreeding like most Syrian Christians."[11] Again, "Chacko said that the high incidence of insanity among Syrian Christians was the price they paid for inbreeding. Mammachi said it wasn't."[12] Chacko's contention records the opinion widely held by educated people, though it need not be the whole truth. Anthropologists dispute the scientific validity of such contention.[13]

Though, the female characters in the novel belong to the same religious group, namely Syrian Christian, they do have differences in age group and they belong to different generations. The novel shows characters belonging to three generations. So the novel has become a record of improvement or otherwise of the social status of women through these generations. What they have attempted and attained, where they have succeeded or failed, how they have rejoiced or suffered—all these things are presented to us as if in a movie. On the whole, the lot of women depicted in the novel leaves us sad but the writer does not seem to be willing to end it with a pessimistic note. That is why despite the tale of 'terror' it unfolds, the novel ends with "naalay" (tomorrow).

Now we proceed to discuss the women characters of the novel. Baby Kochamma is the daughter of Reverend E. John Ipe, who was a priest of the Mar Thoma Church. He had seven children but only two of them survived. Baby Kochamma is one of those survivors, the other being her brother, Benaan John Ipe. Her real name was Navomy Ipe but everybody called her Baby. Her father Reverend John Ipe was well-known as 'Punyan Kunju' and widely respected in the Christian community because at the age of seven, he had been personally blessed by the Patriarch of Antioch, the Sovereign head of the Syrian Christian Church.

It is not strange for the son or daughter of such a man to be attracted to religion. But her family background is not the real reason of her turning to religion in her early life. In fact, she cheats herself and people around her (including her family) by pretending to be religious. Her adventures in the realm of religion are an outcome of a normal, biological impulse which she attempts to promote in a deceptive garb. The attempt fails eventually and the result is she lands in abnormality and perversion.

Early in her life, at the age of eighteen to be accurate, she falls in love with an Irish monk Father Mulligan who comes to her father's house frequently and has his lunch with him. Though her father fails, the Jesuit recognises the sexual excitement in the girl while she hovers around the table.

Then Baby Kochamma tries to seduce Mulligan with "weekly exhibitions of staged charity." As Father Mulligan is expected every Thursday morning, she forcebathes some poor village child with a hard red soap. As Mulligan stops near the well, the young girl asks him to explain some passage of the Bible. So, the Bible is used as a ruse by them "to be with each other" as both of them are "quaking with unchristian passion."

As Father Mulligan has to return to Madras after a year, separation seems inevitable. So, Baby Kochamma resolves to become a Roman Catholic because she thinks it will enable her to be in close contact with Father Mulligan. So, much against the wishes of her father, she converts to Roman Catholic faith and enters a convent in Madras as a trainee novice. But soon she finds the priests and bishops monopolised by senior Sisters with "biblical doubts more sophisticated than hers" and realizes that "it might be years before she got anywhere near Father Mulligan." That makes her "restless and unhappy" and she leaves the convent soon. She refuses, however, to reconvert to Syrian Church.

Her parents could not imagine anything else than marriage for their daughter. But they had conceded to her becoming a nun too. As she leaves the convent, they find a blind alley before her. No man belonging to the Roman Catholic Church can marry an ex-nun and a Syrian Christian cannot many her as she has opted herself out. So, the prospects of her getting married seem nil. Therefore her father decides that there is no harm in getting education and she attends a course of study at the University of Rochester in America. She returns to India two years later with a diploma in Ornamental Gardening.

When she returns from Rochester, she has grown fat. She spends her time at the Ayemenem House in gardening. She does not, however, forget Father Mulligan. She takes care of her body and makes a fresh entry in her diary everyday: I love you I love you. Moreover, she tries to remain in contact with Father Mulligan who too stays in touch with her.

Father Mulligan had begun studying Hindu scriptures to denounce them intelligently but the study eventually leads him to a change of faith. He becomes a Vaishnava and joins an ashram north of Rishikesh. Even then he continues writing to her every Diwali and sends a greeting card every new year. Baby Kochamma preserves such things as objects so dear to her.

The only exception to the rule occurs when he sends her a photograph of himself addressing a gathering of middle class Punjabi widows at a spiritual camp. Obviously, she is jealous of the widows. As Arundhati Roy puts it, "She was offended by the fact that he had actually, eventually, renounced his vows, but not for her.... It was like welcoming someone with open arms, only to have him walk straight past into someone else's."

Then Baby Kochamma comes to know that he is no more. That does not alter the text of the entries in her diary. Her memory of him is now hers, not shared by others. "Savagely, fiercely, hers." She strips him in her imagination of his religious garb and reclothes him in the Coca Cola cassock and comfortable sandals. The death of her beloved does not turn her to a widow-like living. Instead she becomes more concerned about make-up, takes much interest in lotteries and enjoys watching colour TV to such an extent that gardening is totally discarded. She has a new haircut, applies dye and wears a lot of jewellery. In brief she behaves like a teenager at even eighty-three. That is why the novelist remarks: "Baby Kochamma had lived her life backwards. As a young woman she had renounced the material world, and now, as an old one, she seemed to embrace it. She hugged it and it hummed her back."

What we have discussed so far about Baby Kochamma bears out the following:

Firstly, her parents, despite contact with the west, consider marriage as a summum bonum of a woman's life. Education is deemed as a poor substitute for marriage, not as something desirable and valuable for its own sake. Secondly, they are not sensitive to the instincts of young ones. They fail to see through Baby Kochamma's design when she converts to Roman Catholic faith and joins a convent.

Then, Baby Kochamma is a study in hypocrisy and deception. She tries to exploit religion to promote her sexual end. She is honest neither to herself nor to her parents and society. She persuades herself over years "that her unconsummated love for Father Mulligan had been entirely due to her restraint and her determination to do the right thing."[14] The fact, however, remains that she has never asserted her love truthfully, nor ever made an honest approach for its consummation. Thus the sole responsibility for the failure in her love affair lies with herself and there can be no reasonable ground to blame anybody else.

Thirdly, Baby Kochamma is jealous of people who succeed in moving close to Mulligan whether they are monks or nuns. Even the Punjabi widows seem competitors to her and that is why she discards Mulligan's photograph with them. Though religion is often used as camouflage for sex, she seems to project her own feelings to others when she regards them as competitors. Her jealousy, makes her quite inventive when she turns the 'goswamis' into 'co-swamis' which implies that the Vaishnava sadhus are no better than co-husbands (counter-posed to the traditional institution of co-wives) of the female devotees.

Fourthly, Baby Kochamma shows the courage of a rebel when she converts to Roman Catholic faith but she dares not challenge the traditional ideas about love and marriage. She makes a rotten, dishonest compromise with the convention and pays heavily for it—the real happiness eludes her all her life and she remains a spinster.

Her frustration in love and repressed libido provide us with the key to comprehend the cold, calculated and inhuman role she plays in the novel. She has become narcissist and eventually goes to the extent of sadism. Despite her western education and apparent modernisation, she rears all the reactionary ideas inherited from the feudal past in her heart and misses no opportunity to express them violently in word and deed. She is unkind to children, to the lower castes and classes, to Hindus in general and even to women.

She is so concerned with her own dress and appearance that she ignores the occasion and pays no heed to the feelings of the persons around her. Her narcissism proves her worse than the illiterate folk. She goes to attend the funeral of her grand niece Sophie Mol. It is certainly not an occasion of rejoicing and requires no show of pomp. Sensible people wear simple, modest dresses when they are mourning. But the fashionable lady Baby Kochamma attends the funeral clad in an expensive sari! And even at the age of eighty-three, she asks her grand niece, Rahel: "How d'you like my bob?"

It is a pity that she submits in name of decency and honour to the very sexist, casteist and communal prejudices that have stood in her way and denied fulfilment to her. This goes to such an extent that she becomes herself a tool of social oppression. That is a phenomenon that seems strange to us at first sight but is not so rare in society. In fact, it is victims turning the tools of oppression that keeps the wheel moving.

Her hatred for the Hindus is so irrational that her nephew cannot but challenge her remark. So, when she complains that the Hindus "have no sense of privacy," Chacko retorts: "They have horns and scaly skins. And I have heard that their babies hatch from eggs."[15]

Baby Kochamma subscribes to the commonly held view that a married daughter has no position in her parent's home and a divorced one, no position anywhere at all. It becomes worse if the divorce is from a love marriage and worst, if she is divorcee from inter-community marriage.[16] Ammu, according to her, committed a serious offence by marrying a Bengali Hindu and the divorce turned it even more serious. In fact, she is jealous of Ammu for daring to exercise her right to choose the man she marries and to discard him when found unworthy. As the novelist puts it: "Baby Kochamma resented Ammu, because she saw her quarrelling with a fate that she,

Baby Kochamma herself, felt she had graciously accepted. The fate of the wretched Man-less woman. The sad, Father Mulligan-less Baby Kochamma."[17]

Baby Kochamma, like Mammachi, has a double standard in matters regarding sex. What is permitted to man is strictly denied to woman according to her ethics. So Chacko is allowed to carry on his libertine relationships with women in factory and a separate entrance for Chacko's room is built to facilitate it. Baby Kochamma accepts Mammachi's explanation that Chacko has his "Men's Needs" which must be satisfied. She does not find any "contradiction between Chacko's Marxist mind and feudal libido." The only worry she has is about the Naxalites and that for a strange reason: "(they) had been known to force men from Good Families to many servant girls whom they had made pregnant."[18]

Obviously, she does not believe in women's needs or women's rights. That is why she does not bother about the smell of the women Chacko brings to his bedroom but wonders how Ammu can endure the smell of a Paravan. As soon as Ammu's relationship with Velutha is revealed, she locks Ammu and rushes to the police station with a false complaint. Eventually it leads to the death of Velutha and the banishment and dispersal of Ammu and her children. She is responsible for ruining the lives of Ammu (who dies at thirty-one), Estha (who becomes speechless at last) and Rahel (who does not find solace in her life).

Baby Kochamma declares rather stoically after all the mishap: "As ye sow, so shall ye reap." "As though she had nothing to do with the Sowing and Reaping."[19] To say the least, that is outrageous. She is responsible for poisoning the minds of Mammachi and Chacko, for concocting a false case against Velutha, for tricking the children into betraying Velutha, for advising Chacko to return Estha to his father and to ask Ammu to pack her luggage and leave.

Baby Kochamma hates Estha and Rahel because they are half-Hindus born of a love marriage outside community. She subjects them to numerous impositions like speaking in English only, avoiding innocent games like reading backwards and misses no opportunity to punish them. Then, in the name of saving Ammu, she makes Estha identify Velutha as a criminal. A sense of guilt oppresses the soul of the child ever since then and he becomes speechless gradually. Even when Estha and Rahel come back to Ayemenem after twenty-three years, Baby Kochamma does not soften. She is "delighted that Estha had not spoken to Rahel."[20] She does not deem them her responsibility and wants to get rid of them soon. In a shrill, faltering voice she asks Rahel: "What are your plans? How long will you be staying? Have you decided?"[21] Such hardness at the age of eighty-three, when none but a female attendant is left in the house is really striking.

Baby Kochamma has intense hatred for Velutha because he is outcaste and belongs to a group called Paravan. His skill as a carpenter does not seem to be a redeeming factor to her. His union activity and association with the communist party makes him even more pernicious to her. She warns Rahel against being 'over-familiar' with Velutha and she scolds Mammachi too for her indulgence to him.[22] When Baby Kochamma is humiliated by the processionists, she blames Velutha for it.[23] She misses no opportunity to implicate him in a false case and get him killed, therefore, when his relationship with Ammu is revealed.

All she does to Velutha and Ammu is justified on the ground that they had transgressed love laws. But what about herself? She has loved a man—Mulligan—who stands outside caste society. What but his white skin can make him touchable? To love a man who has taken vows to remain celibate is no mean transgression of law but as it remains secret and unconsummated despite attempts to seduce him, she thinks it is okay!

People who betray others cannot trust anyone in life. They are always haunted by the memory of what they have done to others and afraid of being paid back in their own coins. That is true about Baby Kochamma. This is what we find about her in the novel:

> ...Her old fears of the Revolution and the Marxist-Leninist menace had been rekindled by new television worries about the growing number of desperate and dispossessed people. She viewed ethnic cleaning, famine and genocide as direct threats to her furniture.

> She kept her doors and windows locked, unless she was using them. She used windows for specific purposes. For a Breath of Fresh Air. To pay for the Milk. To Let Out a Trapped Wasp (which Kochu Maria was made to chase around the house with a towel).
>
> She even locked, her sad, paint-flaking fridge where she kept her week's supply of cream buns that Kochu Maria brought her from Best bakery in Kottayam. And the two bottles of rice-water that she drank instead of ordinary water. In the shelf below the baffle tray, she kept what was left of Mammachi's willow-pattern dinner-service.
>
> She put the dozen or so bottles of insulin that Rahel brought her in the cheese and butter compartment. She suspected that these days, even the innocent and the round-eyed could be crockery crooks, or cream-bun cravers, or thieving diabetics cruising Ayemenem for imported insulin.
>
> She didn't even trust the twins. She deemed them Capable of Anything. Anything at all....[24]

Baby Kochamma seems detestable to us when we consider her role in the 'terror' that kills Velutha and causes the untimely death of Ammu and ruins the lives of Estha and Rahel. But she is not only a victimizer, a tool of social oppression but she is herself a victim of society. We have to bear in mind how false notions of ideal womanhood are filled in the brains of girls at a tender age. Brainwashed with sexist, casteist, class and communal ideas they become incapable of thinking and acting sanely, even for the sake of their own love and fulfilment. Baby Kochamma's power, prosperity and glamour dissolve in thin air when we realise her defeat and failure in life.

Mammachi is the sister-in-law of Baby Kochamma, the wife of her brother Benaan John Ipe. Her real name is Soshamma but she is generally known as Mammachi while her husband is usually called Pappachi in the novel. Though she is much akin to Baby Kochamma in submitting to the traditional notions of male supremacy, love and marriage, her disposition and lot differs a lot from that of Baby Kochamma.

She is more of a victim because she is married while Baby Kochamma retains a lot of power and privilege at the cost of marriage. Such phenomenon is not unusual in society and several writers have likened marriage to "enclosure" or "prison" for the same reason.

Baby Kochamma suffers because she fails to have the man of her choice. Mammachi has got a husband from arranged marriage seventeen years older than herself belonging to her own country and community. Yet the marriage does not prove happy as her husband develops some disorder in his personality. The novelist goes deep into the roots of that disorder and demonstrates a sound knowledge of problems that haunt the families of the ambitious elite sometime.

Benaan John Ipe was an Imperial Entomologist at Pusa Institute and had become Joint Director, Entomology after independence and retired as a Director. He had discovered a moth belonging to a species and genus hitherto unknown to science, but his claim was dismissed at the time. Twelve years later the fact was admitted but the moth was named after the then Acting Director of the Department of Entomology, a junior officer whom he had always disliked. That hurt him deeply and turned the ill-humoured man more so. He was polite and generous to outsiders but a tormentor to his wife and children.

So, Mammachi is beaten either with a brass vase or an ivory handled riding crop.[25] She becomes used to it and remains a passive sufferer all along. The brutality stops only when Chacko, comes home for a summer vacation from Oxford, intervenes and tells his father: "I never want this to happen again."[26] His father reacts to this by ignoring the plates of food brought to him and by smashing his favourite mahogany rocking chair late at night. He never touches Mammachi again, but neither does he speak to her for the rest of his life. Moreover, whenever the visitors are expected he sits on the verandah and sews buttons that are not missing on to his shirts to create the impression that his wife neglects him. Such double faced men are typical products of our civilization which permits one sort of conduct at home and a different one elsewhere. We often come across men who are kind, generous and polite elsewhere but rude and tyrannical at home. When he dies Mammachi cries not because she loves him but because she has become used to him (as Ammu in the novel puts it).

Mammachi is not only a passive sufferer of her husband's beating, she is a victim of his jealousy also. During the six-month diploma course at Vienna that makes him qualified for the post of Imperial Entomologist, Mammachi takes her first lessons on the violin. Her teacher, Launsky Tieffenthal makes the mistake of telling her husband that she is "exceptionally talented" and "potentially concert class." That leads to an abrupt end of her lessons.[27] Later at Kottayam he breaks the bow of the violin one night and throws it in the river.[28] The same jealousy is expressed again when the pickle making business of Mammachi brings attention to her. Though she is "practically blind," he refuses to help her because pickle-making is not "a suitable job for a high-ranking ex-Government official."[29] Thus, her married life is devoid of love, understanding and co-operation. It means nothing but domination by a bully who lives a bored life himself and bores others too.

Mammachi is hard-working and deserves to be called better at business than her son. She is the founder of the pickle factory and it remains "a small but profitable enterprise" under her.[30] Her son, Chacko, who comes in the garb of a saviour and stops beating, replaces his father's domination with his own in the family. So, he usurps Mammachi's factory, has it registered as a partnership and informs her that she is the sleeping partner. Thus, despite his professed Marxism. Chacko follows Manu and the tradition in asserting the son's domination over mother in old age. Mammachi submits to it as such ideas are so familiar to her.

Mammachi, despite her suffering at the hand of a male chauvinist and sadist husband, loses all our sympathy when we come to consider her attitude to sex in respect of people younger than herself. Her ideas here betray sex bias as well as class bias to an outrageous extent. Her daughter as well as her son is a divorcee but she applies two different norms to their sex-relation. To her son Chacko, she permits "Men's

Needs," and does not mind his flirting with "pretty women who worked in the factory."[31] She goes to the extent of providing a separate entrance to his room at the eastern end of the house "so that the objects of his 'Needs' wouldn't have to go traipsing through the house."[32] Her daughter Ammu, on the other hand, loves a single man but Mammachi resents her 'women's needs.' Her tolerance of 'Men's Needs' as far as her son was concerned, becomes "the fuel for her manageable fury at her daughter."[33] Ammu is locked up in her bedroom, insulted and eventually banished from Ayemenem House. She is accused of having "defiled generations of breeding." It does not occur to her what Chacko has done.

Mammachi appears unkind and unjust to her daughter when she visits Ayemenem fatally ill with asthma and a rattle in her chest. During that last visit Mammachi who has developed a perverse mind, asks her if she has been drinking and suggests that she visit Rahel as seldom as possible.[34] That is highly unbecoming on the part of a mother who has given so much indulgence to her son.

Her attitude toward Margaret shows the same unhealthy bent of her mind. Even before she has seen her, she despises her. Margaret is no better than a 'shopkeeper's daughter' to her. There seems to be no reason for her resentment in fact. "It wasn't just her working class background Mammachi resented. She hated Margaret Kochamma for being Chacko's wife. She hated her for leaving him. But would have hated her even more had she stayed."[35] Obviously, she is jealous, a misanthrope and cannot find pleasure in seeing other women happy.

Her experiences in a world dominated by males and money, her suffering in the enclosure called marriage with a brutish husband have dehumanised her and perverted her mind. That is why she has got a pervert reasoning and a pervert ethics. She slips money secretly to keep the women who satisfy Chacko's 'needs' because "a fee clarified things." She cannot imagine that Margaret has come to her former husband for any other purpose than sex. Margaret is "just another whore" to her and she slips money secretly into the pockets of the dresses she leaves in laundry bin. Margaret remains unaware of the affair as the money is taken away by the dhobi.[36]

Ammu's secret relationship with Velutha is no less natural and justifiable on biological grounds than all the relationships Chacko has with numerous women. Yet Mammachi behaves brutally with Velutha due to caste and class bias. She summons Velutha to her house and then abuses him. Her foul language surprises all the listeners around her. But that is not all: "Mammachi spat into Velutha's face. Thick spit. It spattered across his skin. His mouth and eyes."[37] Mammachi cannot flee her share of responsibility for Velutha's murder by the police as the case against Velutha was not lodged without her consent.

Thus Mammachi is not as crafty as Baby Kochamma but her mind is hardly less pervert than that of Baby Kochamma. She subscribes to the logic and ethics of the male chauvinism in toto. Her conservatism turns her inhuman, nasty and brutish.

Now we come to the third woman in the novel, Ammu. Ammu is the daughter of Benaan John Ipe, the entomologist and represents a new generation which is exposed to new ideas against the former one. Her father is a male chauvinist who makes a lot of distinction between her son and daughter. He sends his son Chacko to Oxford but deems college education "an unnecessary expense for a girl." So she has no choice but to move to Ayemenem from Delhi as her father retired.[38] All she can do next is to wait for marriage according to her father. Thus denied higher education, she remains handicapped in future but shows a lot of independence of mind, courage and moral strength as well as ability to judge people correctly to a certain extent.

At Ayemenem, she helps her mother with house-work and waits for marriage proposals. As her father cannot afford a suitable dowry, marriage proposals do not come. At the same time, she finds living with her parents simply unbearable because her father is an ill-tempered bully who pretends to be an ideal husband and ideal lather before outsiders but makes the life of his family miserable. So Ammu seeks escape from "the clutches of her ill-tempered father and bitter, long-suffering mother."[39] That is why she goes to Calcutta to spend the summer with a distant aunt and ends marrying a Bengali Hindu there.

Her marriage is not based on love, even though the choice is hers. She marries because she does not want to return to Ayemenem. The marriage shows her courage as well as the orthodoxy of her parents. She is daring as she goes against the custom by marrying a person who is neither Christian nor belongs to Kerala. Her parents dislike such inter-community marriage and when she informs them of her decision, they do not reply. Obviously, she transgresses a law according to them by marrying in such unconventional manner.

Ammu shows her strength of mind not only in marrying the man of her choice but also in divorcing him when the choice proves wrong eventually. Her husband, to her dismay, is found to be alcoholic. As he neglects his duty, he is threatened with dismissal by his manager, Mr. Hollick and acquiesces in to his proposal to go away for a while and send his wife to his bunglow to be 'looked after.' When Ammu learns about it, she is stunned at first. But when the unworthy fellow resorts to violence, she does not take it meekly like her mother, Mammachi. She takes the heaviest book from the shelf and hits him with it on head and on legs. She is far from the traditional idea of an ideal woman who worships her husband like a god and obeys him blindly despite all his blemishes.

The divorce leaves her no option but to return unwelcomed to her parents with two children, Estha and Rahel. Her father does not believe her story of the reason for the divorce which implies that she herself is to blame for it. However, his disbelief is not based on his high esteem of her husband, he cannot simply believe that an Englishman can ever covet another man's wife. That vindicates her estimate of her father whom she calls "an incurable British CCP," the CCP being short for chhi-chhi-poach which means shit-wiper in Hindi.

She is equally defiant in her assessment of her brother and dares express her views courageously. She challenges her mother's obsession with her son and refuses to admit that Chacko is "brilliant," "made of prime ministerial material" or "one of the cleverest men in India." She cuts Chacko to size. While her mother and aunt subscribe to the male chauvinist notions of "Men's Needs," she takes a correct view of the self-proclaimed Marxist Chacko and his relationship with women workers of the factory. She is quite accurate in calling it "all hogwash" and characterising him as an "Oxford avatar of the old zamindar mentality—a landlord forcing his attentions on women who depended on him for livelihood."[40] It is significant because others in the novel fail to notice the contrast between the Marxist mind and feudal libido. When Chacko claims to be writing a family biography that the family would have to pay him not to publish, Ammu declares that he is the only person in the family fit for such a biographical blackmail.[41]

Ammu challenges the androcentric notions of society when she avoids surname after divorce. Estha and Rahel have no surname because Ammu is considering reverting to her maiden name, though she feels that choosing between her husband's name and her father's name does not "give a woman much of a choice."[42] Law does not give a daughter any claim to property. Though she does as much work as Chacko, the latter feels free to declare the factory as his own. He tells her children that they have no locus standi and tells her, "What's yours is mine and what's mine is also mine." Ammu views this all as a product of "our wonderful male chauvinistic society."[43]

She is bitterly aware of the hypocrisy around her and she has learned "to recognize and despise the ugly face of sympathy." During the first few months of her stay at the parental home, old female relations pay overnight trips to Ayemenem pretending to show their sympathy for her about her divorce. Actually it is their way of getting devilish pleasure by subjecting her to mental torture systematically. She restrains her dislike and anger with a lot of effort.[44]

As a mother, she loves her children. She is concerned about their innocence which makes them willing to love people who do not love them. That exasperates her. They appear to her like "small bewildered frogs...lolloping arm in arm down a high way full of hurtling traffic." She is "quick to reprimand her children, but even quicker to take offence on their behalf."[45] She wants to impart not only the bookish knowledge to them but cares to teach them correct manners too. That is why she says to Rahel on a certain occasion: "I never want to hear you discussing people's deaths with them again."[46] On another occasion, she makes Rahel realise that careless words hurt people.[47] To the last of her days she cherishes the idea of reliving with her children (whom ill-luck has snatched away from her) in a little house and buying gifts for them. Her children love her no less. Rahel's list of her dear ones places Ammu at the top.[48] And both Estha and Rahel fall in the trap of Baby Kochamma simply because they think it will save Ammu.[49]

The rebel in Ammu does not permit her to remain contented with motherhood and divorceehood. There is an 'unsafe edge,' an 'unmixable mix,' 'the rage of a suicide bomber' along with the 'infinite tenderness of motherhood' in her. So she proceeds to reclaim her body. Her walk changes, she wears flowers in her hair, she spends hours on the riverbank listening to a transistor, smokes cigarettes and has midnight swims.[50] Tired of the proprietary handling of her, she examines her body in bathroom mirror which shows her worry about her passing youth.[51] Then there are other factors which stir her. The dream of the one armed man suggests her that it is no use seeking perfection in life, the small and powerless people like her can but satisfy themselves with the little time provides them.[52] The arrival of Margaret Kochamma provokes her desires.[53] And finally Velutha's return after many years makes her take a fatal decision to "love by night the man her children loved by day."[54] The secret love affair goes on for thirteen days until it is reported to Mammachi by Velutha's father and compounded by the accidental death of Sophie Mol. The briefest comment on the episode seems to be that of the novelist herself: "Biology designed the dance. Terror timed it."[55] To that we can only add that Velutha appears like a father figure to her children and his real love for the children builds a bridge for the love she too needs. But earlier she is drawn to him when she sees him holding a red flag at the procession because he seems to be a rebel, housing "a living, breathing anger against the smug, ordered world" she too resents.[56] So what seems an illicit relationship between a divorcee, touchable woman and an untouchable Paravan is actually a union of two rebels protesting against hypocritical laws of society not in word, but in deed.

When that relationship is revealed, Mammachi and Baby Kochamma who have not only tolerated but assisted Chacko in his licentious affairs with working women, become highly indignant. Ammu is tricked into her bedroom and locked while Velutha is implicated in false cases of attempted rape, kidnapping of children and murder of Sophie Mol. Velutha is grabbed by the police and killed, while she is allowed to attend Sophie's funeral standing separately with her children.[57] Soon after the funeral she goes to the police station and tries to set the record straight. But the police officer dismisses her pleas with the remark that the Kottayam police does not take statement from Veshyas (Prostitutes) and their illegitimate children. He stares at her breasts while speaking, taps them with his baton and asks her to leave quietly.[58] That shows her moral courage on the one hand and the obscene nature of the enforcers of law and order on the other. The incident, however, frightens Baby Kochamma who has not taken into account "the unsafe edge in Ammu" and she contrives to get her out of Ayemenem soon lest the case of Velutha is reopened.[59] So four days after the funeral, Chacko assumes the role of a defender of morality and asks Ammu to pack-up and leave: "Get out of my house before I break every bone in your body."[60]

The punishment is unjust as it ruins three lives for the supposed offence of one. Ammu is separated from her children as Estha is returned to his father and Rahel alone is permitted to live at Ayemenem but Ammu is not allowed to visit her frequently. The last time she comes to Ayemenem and meets Rahel, she has asthma and a rattle in her chest. Desperately wanting to have a good job that enables her to bring her children with her, she tries a number of jobs and dies alone in the Bharat Lodge in Aleppy where she has gone for a job interview.[61]

Before her death, she is haunted by a recurrent dream which springs from her traumatic experience. In that dream, the policemen approach her with snacking scissors, wanting to hack off her hair. "They did that in Kottayam to prostitutes whom they'd caught in the bazaar—branded them so that everybody would know them for what they were. Veshyas. So that new policemen on the beat would have no trouble identifying whom to harass."[62] Obviously, that is related to the shock she has received at the Kottayam police station. Death does not end the humiliation of the unfortunate Ammu: "The Church refused to bury Ammu. On several counts. So Chacko hired a van to transport the body to the electric crematorium. He had her wrapped in a dirty bed sheet and laid out on a stretcher." Finally, she is reduced to ashes and a receipt is given, Receipt No. Q 498673."[63]

Thus Ammu is "humiliated and cornered by her father, illtreated and betrayed by her husband, insulted by the police and rendered destitute by her brother" as Mohit Kumar Ray puts it.[64] If they are men who concede no rights to a woman as daughter, wife, sister and citizen, what can we say about "the long-suffering mother" Mammachi who has not left a soft corner for her miserable daughter in her heart and about the wretched "Man-less" Baby Kochamma who plays a major role in tormenting Ammu and her dear ones? The novelist is, obviously a realist who refuses to pick up male characters alone to malign and glorify the woman. Ammu is a tragic figure who fights powerful tyrannical forces against her and meets an untimely death at the age of thirty-one. When we compare and contrast her with Chacko, we cannot but realise the truth of what Emma Goldman wrote in her 'Women and Other Essays on Feminism': "Society considers the sex experiences of man as attributes of his general development, while similar experiences in life of a woman are looked upon as a terrible calamity, a loss of honour and all that is good and noble in a human being."

Ammu's daughter Rahel too deserves our attention. The novel deals with the story of her life only to the age of thirty-one and most of that story belongs to her childhood. So she deserves to be treated in the following chapter. Therefore, we confine us to a few words about her adult life here. For the sake of convenience, we assume the adult life to begin with the finishing of schooling.

Deserted by father and separated from mother (who dies soon), she is neglected by her maternal uncle, grand mother and grandaunt. The neglect has accidentally resulted in a "release of the spirit." She has grown independent, daring and capable of taking initiative.

After finishing schooling, she gets herself admitted to a college of architecture in Delhi. The decision is·taken not out of interest in architecture but simply because she finds it easy to get herself admitted. Obviously it is her way to stay away from Ayemenem where she is unwanted. She spends eight years in the college without finishing the five-year undergraduate course and taking her degree. The reason given by the novelist shows she is more concerned about living somehow at her own than hoping to build a good career: "The fees were low and it wasn't hard to scratch out a living in the subsidized student mess, rarely going to class, working instead as a draughtsman in gloomy architectural firms that exploited cheap student labour to render their presentation drawings and to blame when things went wrong."[65] She writes occasionally to Chacko and Mammachi, but does not return to Ayemenem.

During her slay at the School of Architecture, she meets Larry McCaslin in Delhi and marries him. Though the decision is hers, it is not taken under ideal conditions. She is aware of the fact that she has no locus standi at Ayemenem, that there is nobody to arrange marriage and pay a dowry for her.[66] So she drifts into marriage "like a passenger drifts towards an occupied chair in an airport lounge with a Sitting Down sense."[67]

This marriage, like that of her mother and uncle is outside her community. Larry is an American research scholar in Indian architecture and so her choice is socially acceptable. Larry is not a male chauvinist but the marriage proves prosaic. Larry values her but fails to understand her. He is at a loss to decide what he sees in her eyes and places it somewhere between indifference and despair.[68] Rahel refuses to continue the relationship when she realises its futility. Marriage to her is not a yoke. So she breaks it soon. Evidently, she has a clarity of perception and confidence which surpasses that of her mother. She does not feel shame or moral weakness for the divorce and informs Comrade Pillai about it without least hesitation. Instead, it is Pillai who is shocked:

"We are divorced," Rahel hoped to shock him into silence.

> "Die-vorced?" His voice rose to such a high register that it cracked on the question mark. He even pronounced the word as though it were a form of death.[69]

The divorce does not leave her depressed. She works as a waitress in an Indian restaurant in New York. And then she serves as a night clerk in a bullet-proof cabin at a gas station outside Washington. The job requires a lot of patience and courage because she has to witness drunks, pimps and criminals so often.[70]

Rahel has a great sense of responsibility for her brother Estha, who is a part of her own self to her. So as soon as she learns from Baby Kochamma's letter that Estha has been re-returned, she leaves her job at the gas station and leaves America gladly for Ayemenem. Unlike her divorcee mother, she has no burden of children with her. But she has to look after her brother, Estha whom traumatic experiences of life have turned speechless.

We may conclude our appraisal of Rahel with the remarks of a notable critic Mohit Kumar Ray: "Rahel understands her mother better than Ammu ever could her mother. There is enough evidence in the novel that she shares the agony of her mother, realizes the great injustice and cruelty done on her mother, and is filled with profound compassion for her mother. Her mother has always remained a living presence in her memory. Seen from the feminine perspective, the novel records a progress, albeit slow, in feminism, offer some rays of hope and seems to suggest a distinct possibility of redemption."[71]

A few words about Kochu Maria will not be out of place here. Kochu Maria is the cook who has been serving the Ayemenem House since the days of Benaan John Ipe. She is a Syrian Christian proud of her social status and very keen to assert it. She draws a salary of seventy five rupees a month.[72] That too is divested by her truck driver brother-in-law who comes to Ayemenem House for the purpose.[73]

She is old-fashioned and wears half-sleeved white chatta with a V-neck and white mundu, folded like a crish cloth fan behind her. She has to wear a housemaid's apron inside the house. She has "short thick forearms and fleshy nose with flared nostrils." Deep folds of skin connect her nose to either side of the chin and her head is too large for her body.[74]

She is illiterate and ignorant. That has contributed a lot to her suspiciousness. She is "wary of other people's versions of the outside world."[75] She does not believe Rahel when she tells her that an American called Neil Armstrong has walked on the moon. There may be Americans and one of them may have an absurd name like that but she can not concede that he has walked on the moon.[76]

She is foolish enough to take offence at the innocent plays of children. When Estha says "Et tu? Brute? Then fall Ceasar!," she asks him to go to his father's house with his mother where he can break as many beds as he likes.[77] That is audacious too as she is simply a housemaid. In her folly, she believes that 'Et tu, Kochu Maria' means something like 'Kochu Maria, you ugly black dwarf and the child is insulting her in English.[78]

She seems to be mischievous by nature and zealous in carrying out the evil designs of her employers. She serves Mammachi well when Mammachi asks her to examine the bed-sheets of Margaret.[79] She attends Baby Kochamma as her "midget lieutenant" in getting Ammu locked in her bedroom.[80] Lastly, she is the only companion of the television addict Baby Kochamma after the death of Mammachi and departure of Chacko. It is almost a poetic justice that Baby Kochamma at eighty-three finds no human company than the illiterate and ignoble Kochu Maria.

What emerges from the above study is that the novel with the three women Baby Kochamma, Mammachi and Ammu presents a perfect trio of suffering women. Baby Kochamma, herself a victim of social prejudices is conditioned by society and identifies herself with the ideas and forces of oppression. Mammachi is dehumanised and her mind becomes twisted as a result of suffering in a society dominated by men and money. Ammu, on the other hand, is the rebel who represents the defiance of the present state of society from educated, passionate and thinking women. She stands for those women who are aspiring for freedom and equality. This section of women is challenging traditional ideas and conventions. The hopes for the future lie with this section only. The other section consists of decadent elements like Baby Kochamma and Kochu Maria. They are satisfied (we wonder really!) with their present, and they become consumerists who care little about fellow beings. They are television addicts caring for nothing but life-styles. Obviously, they hold no hope for the future. Despite possessing and using latest products of modern science and technology, they are not leading the society forward. To use the words of Arundhati Roy, they are living their lives backwards.

REFERENCES

1. Shastri, Shakuntala Rao, *Women in the Sacred Laws*, Bombay, 1959, 189.
2. Briffault, Robert, *The Mothers: A study of the Origin of Sentiments and Institutions*, New York, 1952, Vol. I, 345; for the original text, *vide*, *Manusmriti* (V. 147-148).
3. *Social Welfare*, Vol. XXXIV, No. 11-12, Feb.-March, 1993.
4. Kudchedkar, Shirin, & Al-Issa, Sabiha, (ed.), *Violence Against Women, Women Against Violence*, Delhi, 1998, 90.
5. *Ibid.*, 144.
6. *India Today*, Dec. 20, 1999.
7. Chaitanya, Krishna, *Kerala*, New Delhi, 1972, 58-60.
8. Roy, Arundhati, *The God of Small Things*, London, 1998, 33.
9. *Ibid.*, 66.
10. *Ibid.*, 170.
11. *Ibid.*, 64.
12. *Ibid.*, 223.
13. Reed, Evelyn, *Woman's Evolution*, New York, 3rd Printing, 1975, 7-8.
14. Roy, Arundhati, *Op. cit.*, 45.
15. *Ibid.*, 86.
16. *Ibid.*, 45.
17. *Ibid.*
18. *Ibid.*, 168.
19. *Ibid.*, 31.
20. *Ibid.*, 20.
21. *Ibid.*, 29.
22. *Ibid.*, 184.
23. *Ibid.*, 80-81.
24. *Ibid.*, 28-29.
25. *Ibid.*, 50 & 181

26. Roy, Arundhati, *Op. cit.*, 48.
27. *Ibid.*, 50.
28. *Ibid.*, 48.
29. *Ibid.*, 47.
30. *Ibid.*, 57.
31. *Ibid.*, 65.
32. *Ibid.*, 168-169.
33. *Ibid.*, 258.
34. *Ibid.*, 159-161.
35. *Ibid.*, 167-168.
36. *Ibid.*, 169.
37. *Ibid.*, 284.
38. *Ibid.*, 38.
39. *Ibid.*, 39.
40. *Ibid.*, 65.
41. *Ibid.*, 38.
42. *Ibid.*, 36-37.
43. *Ibid.*, 41.
44. *Ibid.*, 42.
45. *Ibid.*, 43.
46. *Ibid.*, 50.
47. *Ibid.*, 112.
48. *Ibid.*, 151.
49. *Ibid.*, 318.
50. *Ibid.*, 44.
51. *Ibid.*, 222.
52. *Ibid.*, 217.
53. *Ibid.*, 340.
54. *Ibid.*, 44.
55. *Ibid.*, 335.
56. *Ibid.*, 176.
57. *Ibid.*, 5.
58. *Ibid.*, 8.
59. *Ibid.*, 321.
60. *Ibid.*, 225.
61. *Ibid.*, 159-161.
62. *Ibid.*, 161.
63. *Ibid.*, 162-163.
64. Dhawan, R.K., (ed.), *Arundhati Roy The Novelist Extraordinary*, New Delhi. 1999, 54.

65. Roy, Arundhati, *Op. Cit.,* 17-18.
66. *Ibid.,* 17.
67. *Ibid.,* 18.
68. *Ibid.,* 19.
69. *Ibid.,* 130.
70. *Ibid.,* 20.
71. Dhawan, R.K. *Op. Cit.,* 60.
72. Roy, Arundhati, *Op. Cit.,* 170.
73. *Ibid.,* 295.
74. *Ibid.,* 170.
75. *Ibid.*
76. *Ibid.,* 171.
77. *Ibid.,* 83.
78. *Ibid.,* 171.
79. *Ibid.,* 169.
80. *Ibid.,* 258.

4

THE CHILDREN IN THE NOVEL

Children are also included in the "small things" Arundhati Roy cares for. Such a concern is not so unexpected as she is the daughter of a Christian mother and Christianity is well-known for its glorification of childhood. For example, we find the following in the *Bible*:

> And they brought young children to him, that he should touch them: and his disciples rebuked those that brought them.
>
> But when Jesus saw it, he was much displeased, and said unto them, suffer the young children to come unto me, and forbid them not: for of such is the kingdom of God.
>
> Verily I say unto you, whosoever shall not receive the kingdom of God as a little child, he shall not enter therein.
>
> And he took them up in his arms, put his hands upon them, and blessed them.
>
> (*St. Mark*, X. 13-16)

As the above passage quoted from the *New Testament* shows (a variant of which is also available in *St. Luke,* chap. XVIII, 15-17), Jesus Christ viewed children as embodiment of innocence. Similar attitude can be found in the lives and teachings of the persons who have influenced the course of history through the ages.

Political leaders in different countries, while differing in their political convictions and speaking different languages, do not dispute the fact that children represent the future of the society and as such, deserve love and care. We read and hear a lot about their concern for children.

That is true about the leaders of India as well. Mahatma Gandhi who led the national movement in the country for over two decades was well known for his fondness for children. Nehru, the first Prime Minister of India, liked to be called 'uncle' by children. We can add so many names if we like, but that does not seem necessary.

It is but natural, then, that the *Constitution* of India that came in force with effect from January 26, 1950 pays heed to children and seeks to defend their interests.

Part III of the *Constitution* deals with the fundamental rights of the citizens. It contains certain articles which are relevant in this respect.

Article 23 (1) is not meant for children only, it prohibits "traffic in human beings and begar and other similar forms of forced labour" in general. Obviously, it applies to children too.

Article 24 says: "No child below the age of fourteen years shall be employed to work in any factory or mine or engaged in any other hazardous employment."

Besides the fundamental rights, the *Constitution* mentions certain other policies which the state is expected to pursue, though the courts cannot compel it to implement them. They are called 'Directive Principles of State Policy' and placed in the Part IV of the *Constitution*.

Here too, we find clauses (e) and (f) of article 39 referring to children. The relevant portion of the article states: "The state shall, in particular, direct its policy towards securing— (e) that the health and strength of workers, men and women, and the tender age of children are not abused and that citizens are not forced by economic necessity to avocations unsuited to their age or strength; (f) that children are given opportunities and facilities to develop in a healthy manner and in conditions of freedom and dignity and that childhood and youth are protected against exploitation and against moral and material abandonment."

The clause (f) was added to the article by the Forty-second Amendment Act of 1976 and came into effect from Jan. 1, 1977.

Article 45 included in the 'Directive Principles of State Policy' goes on to declare:

"The state shall endeavour to provide, within period of ten years from the *Constitution,* for free and compulsory education for all children until they complete the age of fourteen years."

Besides the constitutional provisions, we find a number of laws meant to protect children. The Indian Factories Act of 1881 imposed a minimum age limit of seven years for employment. The Factories Act as amended in 1922 raised the age limit to fifteen years. The Indian Mines Act of 1923 raised the minimum age for employment in mines to thirteen years.

The Employment of Children Act (1938) was the first Act devoted entirely to child labour. The Act exempted family-run workshops and listed occupations and processes in which children could not be employed. The Factories Act of 1948 set fourteen as the minimum age for employment in factories. A fitness certificate from a doctor was required for children between fourteen to eighteen. The number of continuous hours of work, night work and the use of machinery by young persons were restricted. The law defined factory as a premise where manufacturing was carried with the aid of power employing at least ten persons, and that employing more than twenty where no power was used.

More laws were enacted after the *Constitution* came into force. The Plantation Labour Act of 1951 prohibited the employment of children under twelve. The Mines Act of 1952 laid the minimum age-limit as fifteen. The Factories Act of 1954 laid the minimum age-limit as seventeen for workers at night. The Beedi and Cigar Workers Act of 1960 prohibited the employment of children below fourteen in beedi and cigar manufacturing factories. Besides these central government laws, the state governments passed Acts regulating the employment in hotels, restaurants and shops. These Acts set age-limits between twelve to fifteen for different occupations.

Now let us turn to reality from legal provisions and promises. Childhood is supposed to be a period when young ones are expected to live a carefree life. It is the duty of their elders to look after them, to provide them with nourishing food and necessary clothes, to care for their health and education, to pay proper attention to their emotional needs. Childhood is a period of growth and development. It is also traditionally associated with joy and play.

The picture is not, unfortunately, as rosy as it is fancied to be. We are living in a society divided in classes and the conditions vary from class to class. There are bound to be some differences. We have to be aware of the fact in any examination of the social conditions, though there may be certain things applicable to all classes. We can remember well, in this connection, what Tolstoy wrote at the very beginning of *Anna Karenina*: "All happy families resemble one another; every unhappy family is unhappy in its own way." So the children too may be similar in happiness but differing in their unhappiness. That is what we deem necessary to find out and record.

The children of the upper classes are, generally speaking lucky in as much as their guardians can afford good food, good clothes, toys, medicine and education for them. Children in such families are not in fact victims of poverty. They suffer from the ill-temper, obsessions or prejudices of their elders. Sometimes either or both of the parents are careless and pay little attention to their children. They think their responsibility ends with getting them admitted to schools or colleges and spending money for them. At times the relations between the parents are strained and that too tells upon the mental health of children. If one or both of the parents are dead, children become unwanted dependents on the relations who feel free to exploit and maltreat them. Quarrels, litigations and intrigues for property in a big family leave the young ones with a feeling of insecurity and sometimes endanger their lives too. Such unhappy experiences of childhood haunt the memory of people in advanced age too sometimes and make them mentally ill. The children of widows and divorcees are usually destined to suffer in our society.

The lot of the children of the poor families is far worse than that. Their guardians are simply unable to provide them properly. So they suffer from malnutrition and education and medical care are luxuries to them. Instead of spending their days in play and learning, they begin to work at an early age. That is why the *Constitution* felt obliged to take note of the child labour and expressed its good will for them. Several central and state legislations too had to take note of them.

Despite all that a considerable part of the children stay at home to care for cattle, tend young children, collect firewood and work in the fields. They are also employed in cottage industries, tea stalls, restaurants or serve as household workers. Some of them take to begging or picking rags and bottles for resale. Then a section of them serves as bonded labourers for money lenders. The 1981 census reported that 82.2 million of India's 158.8 million children (ages six to fourteen) did not attend school. Only 52.2 million of India's 123.7 million rural children (ages six to fourteen) were in school (34.4 million boys, 17.4 million girls). In urban India 24.4 million of 35.1 million attended school (13.5 million boys, 10.9 million girls).

The government is not unaware of the facts as evident from the report of the Committee on Child Labour (1979), a committee appointed by Government of India. The Labour Ministry has admitted quite frankly that "despite the provisions of restrictive labour laws, the practice (of child labour) continues unabated because exploitation of children is of financial advantage to employees and an economic compulsion to the parents."[1] Proceeding with the admission of the "harsh reality," the state has since sought not to abolish child labour but to "ameliorate" the condition of working children as evident from Child Labour (Prohibition and Regulation) Act, 1987 which imposes no age limit on the employment of children but simply prohibits their employment in certain occupations and processes and even that restriction is carefully circumscribed.[2]

While more than half of the children of school going age are undoubtedly not attending school, the estimates vary as to how many of them are working. The 1981 census reported 13.6 million of them or 7.6 per cent of the age-group five to fourteen as working. National Sample Survey put the figure in 1983 as 17.4 million while Operations Research Group of Baroda sponsored by the Labour Ministry found it not less than 44 million. Even the Census reports admit an increase in the number and percentage of the child labour. While 10.7 million or 4.6 per cent of all children were reported working in 1971, there were 13.6 million or 5.2 per cent of them in 1981.[3] Thus there is little reason to hope that the child labour in India will come to an end in course of time without social action and state intervention.

Child labour is allowed to continue as the state, the politicians and the social workers find no other way for poor parents. The laws meant to ameliorate the lot of working children contain loopholes which make it easy for the employers to violate them. Cottage industries are a sacred cow to the government, politicians and social workers as Mahatma Gandhi sought to promote them so zealously. So the cottage industries are left out of the purview of the laws. Then, the factories keep their child labour off during the rare visits of the factory inspectors. Again, there are technicalities like the definition of a factory that enable the employers to evade the laws. Though the laws do not permit children to work in hazardous occupations and processes, they are doing precisely that in glass, bangles and match-producing concerns and their condition in carpet industry is far from satisfactory. The government officials are practical men who do not want to abolish jobs and the unpalatable truth about their condition is hardly made public. For example, the Harbans Singh Report on the condition of working children in the match industry of Sivakasi was never released to the public, because they did not want to abolish twenty thousand jobs.[4]

Only a few of the children who go to school are able to continue and complete their primary education. Estimates about drop out vary. J.P. Naik opined in 1975 that only 40 per cent of the children enrolled in class I, reached class V and about 25 per cent reached class VIII.[5] Subsequent estimates tend to put the percentage much lower. The drop out rate is explained by the fact that most of the primary schools are crowded and face problems like paucity of teachers, and lack of equipment. They can not even seat all their students and provide them with minimum requirements like water and lavatory. Then while the government has abolished tuition fees and supplies free text books to the students in a state like West Bengal, the guardians have to bear the rising cost of the stationery goods. Moreover, the children are pressed hard to purchase several help books and to attend to the private tutors. The guardians who cannot afford it, have to pull out their children.

As for the promise given in the Article 45 of the *Constitution,* more than fifty years instead often have passed since it came into force but "free and compulsory education for all children" below fourteen remains a dream. Several states have made education free up to varying levels but it can not be claimed that education for children below fourteen is free now in almost every state. There are also incentives like midday meals or free ration for school going students. But these benefits are outweighed by other factors mentioned above.

The idea of compulsory education does not find favour with the state, educationsists, social workers or political parties now. Most of them are opposed to compulsion as it smacks of violence. Secondly, it seems detrimental to the interest of the poor parents who need the help of their children to supplement the meagre income of their family and feel unable to bear the expenses of educating their children. It is hoped against hope that the incomes of these parents will rise and they will be able to send their children to school. Myron Weiner in his *The Child and The Stale in India* does not agree with such argument and pleads strongly for state intervention.[6]

While discarding the idea of compulsory education, the schemes of non-formal education for working children have been put forth as a consoling substitute. Experience shows that such schemes bear as dubious results as literacy campaigns and adult education schemes for working people sponsored by the government. Apart from the attitude of the teachers who are not always sincere, the response of the potential learners too contributes to the failure of such schemes. After the hard work of the day, the working children like the rest of the workers are in no mood of attending classes. They want rest and recreation.

Even though the state keeps "free and compulsory education" at bay in the name of non-violence, the children are not spared of violence in our society. They are subjected to violence of both types, namely, structural and behavioural.

The difference between two types is best explained by former [Massachusetts prison official and writer, Dr. James Milligan:

> "By structural violence I mean the increased rates of death and disability suffered by those who occupy the bottom rungs of society, as contrasted by those who are above them. The excess deaths (or at least a demonstrably large proportion of them) are a function of the class structure; and that structure is itself a product of society's collective human choices, concerning how to distribute the collective wealth of the society. These are not acts of god. I am contrasting 'structural' with 'behavioural' violence 'by which I mean the non-natural deaths and injuries that are caused by specific behavioural actions of individuals against individuals, such as the deaths we attribute to homicide, suicide, soldiers in warfare, capital punishment, and so on (spellings as in the original text)."[7]

Milligan illustrates his concept of structural violence with facts which are startling but true:

> "Every fifteen years, on the average, as many people die because of relative poverty as would be killed in a nuclear war that caused 232 million deaths, and every single year, two to three times as many people die from poverty throughout the world as were killed by the Nazi genocide of the Jews over a six-year period. This is, in effect, the equivalent of an on-going, unending, in fact accelerating, thermonuclear war, or genocide on the weak and poor every year of every decade throughout the world."[8]

Children of the poor fall easy prey to structural violence. It is difficult to say how many of them die of malnutrition and anemia because it is deemed unpatriotic to record and report such cases to the press. Similarly the number of children who die of various diseases without receiving any medical care is considerably high but no figures are available to us. Mostly the ignorance and superstition of the parents or guardians is blamed for untimely deaths. But what can the persons having no access to costly medicine and doctors do but console their helpless families with magic water or magic oil? There are organisations in West Bengal and Kerala dedicated to the cause of uprooting superstitions, but their efforts have borne little fruit as there are no hospitals in several localities and if there are, either doctor or medicine is missing. That is hardly an ideal condition for making people science-oriented or to save lives.

Children are subjected to behavioural violence at home, at school, in the locality and if they are working, at their places of work. Rarely such cases reach the press. Children are generally beaten by ill-tempered and alcoholic elders at home. It makes no news as it is deemed as the normal, private business of the family. But the victims become either diffident or rebellious. Some cases of children getting seriously injured and hospitalised have appeared in press during the last decade. As they involved teachers, they indicated a deplorable trend in certain institutions. Children serve as bonded labourers in certain industries and they are subjected to threats, assault and confinement by the goons of the employers. Those employed as household workers fare no better. Several cases of beating and even branding are reported to the press.

The cases reported involve strangely enough, people of respectable families. A few years ago, a female household worker was branded by a woman employed in telephone department. Quite recently, Sister Franceska of the Missionaries of Charity was reported to have branded four girls of Mahatma Gandhi Welfare Centre, Calcutta as they were suspected to have stolen an amount of Rs. 450/- only. The report appeared on the 21st of September, 2000 in the Dainik Basumati on page 1.

Child abuse, the term so much used in sociological discussions, is but the other name of behavioural violence against children. It includes intimidation, swearing, assault and exploitation of children. Discussions about these are generally permitted in the society. But the sexual abuse of children has remained a taboo for long. A few authors who dared to raise the issue were denounced as unhealthy writers and attempts were made to suppress their works. A change for the better seems to have begun now as a recent publication *Bitter Chocolate* seeks to highlight that evil in India. Let us hope the author is not condemned as a promoter of immorality as they would have said in 1940s and 1950s.

The above discussion makes it clear that while we speak of high ideals, our society closes its eyes to child abuse in various forms and shows a callous attitude to children in general. While Arundhati Roy does not present the lot of poor children in India, she does, indeed, highlight this general attitude of callousness, insensitivity and indifference.

The God of Small Things does not depict the lot of many children. There are only three children in the novel, namely, Sophie Mol, Estha and Rahel. The novel presents, as we shall see, a contrast between the first one and the last two. All the three have certain similarities. Their parents are divorced and one of them is not a Syrian Christian. That is what is common to them all. But they differ in several respects too. Sophie Mol's mother is a white woman while the father of Estha and Rahel is a non-white man (Indian and Bengali). While Sophie Mol's father is willing to receive her and her mother gladly and his family is equally enthusiastic about it, Estha and Rahel are forsaken by their father. Sophie Mol is elder than her cousins. A major difference lies in the fact that Sophie Mol dies soon after her arrival as she meets an accident. Estha and Rahel face several odds but survive. The novel can be viewed as a tale of "terror" that destroyed the lives of Velutha and Ammu, but also as a tale of how Estha and Rahel survived.

Estha and his sister are not poor, working class children who get their childhood lost in early struggle for survival. They are not subjected to malnutrition, nor denied medical care and education. Their problems are related not to body, but to mind. Their suffering belongs to their psyche and their tragedy is spiritual rather than physical or material. That is especially true about Estha who suffers the most.

Estha's parents were not poor. His father was an assistant manager in a tea estate in Assam while his mother's parental home had a pickle factory. So Estha had a bourgeois background on both sides. He and his sister are subjected to adversity as their parents get divorced and his mother comes to her parental home with two children where they are quite unwanted. Even then, they acquire good education in English and some "pocket money" which is inconceivable to poor children of their age. The children of the poor have to earn, beg or steal to get even a trivial amount in their pockets. So Estha's problem is a product of circumstances.

Estha had an unhappy childhood because his father's "drunken violence followed by post-drunken badgering" began when he was barely two. "When his bouts of violence began to include the children, and the war with Pakistan began, Ammu left her husband and returned, unwelcome to her parents in Ayemenem."[9] That is, Estha was only five at that time.

At Ayemenem the children along with their mother were unwanted, a fact the children in their innocence could not realize instantly. Their "wide-eyed vulnerability and their willingness to love people who did not really love them" exasperated Ammu and "sometimes made her want to hurt them—just as an education, a protection."[10]

However, Estha and her sister soon came to know what people around them thought about them. They had a double stigma of mixed parentage attached to them, both religious (because their father was Hindu and mother Syrian Christian) and ethnic (their father being a Bengali and mother, a Keralite). Moreover, they were the children of a divorced daughter who had no locus standi. Their grand aunt soon let them know it. Baby Kochamma disliked the twins, for she considered them doomed, fatherless waifs. Worse still, they were Half-Hindu Hybrids whom no self-respecting-Syrian Christian would ever marry. She was keen for them to realize that they (like herself) lived on sufferance in the Ayemenem House, their maternal uncle's house, where they really had no right to be."[11] His maternal uncle Chacko too does not hesitate to tell the children "that human Ammu had no Locusts·Stand I" (a funny way of putting *locus standi*).[12]

Then there is another occasion when Chacko tells Ammu that the children are not his responsibilities but "millstone around his neck." A sensitive boy like Estha could not dismiss that lightly. "Estha knew about millstones. In Mutiny on the Bounty, when people died on sea, they were wrapped in white sheets and thrown overboard with millstones around their necks so that the corpses wouldn't float. Estha wasn't sure how they decided how many millstones to take with them before they set off on their voyage."[13]

As if that is not enough, Kochu Maria (the maid servant of the house) too finds an opportunity to remind Estha of his position in the house:

At night, Estha would stand on his bed with his sheet wrapped around him and say, "Et tu? Brute?—Then fall Caesar!" and crash into bed without bending his knees, like a stabbed corpse. Kochu Maria, who slept on the floor on a mat, said that she would complain to Mammachi.

'Tell your mother to take you to your father's house,' she said, 'There you can break as many beds as you like. These are not your beds. This isn't your house.'[14]

While Estha is agonised by the coldness of his relations at Ayemenem, the separation of his parents has created a feeling of insecurity and uncertainty, an identity crisis. His mother has not chosen a surname as yet[15] and the result is that on his note book "Estha had rubbed out his surname with spit, and taken half of the paper with it. Over the whole mess, he had written in pencil un-known."[16] The behaviour shows not only worry but also resentment for his father.

At Ayemenem, Baby Kochamma grudges his "moments of high happiness" and the comfort the twins "drew from each other."[17] Baby Kochamma's Australian missionary friend, Miss Mitten too complains about his rudeness and his habit of reading backwords. "She told Baby Kochamma that she had seen Satan" in his eyes.[18] Baby Kochamma herself later observes: "They're sly. They're uncouth. Deceitful. They're growing wild."[19] Even Ammu who loves him so much fears he may become a "male chauvinist pig" one day, an apprehension based on the evolution of her own brother Chacko.[20] Needless to say these observations are belied by the turn of the events.

The unhappy boy had got some comfort as he had discovered a man, Velutha who really loved the twins. Gradually he had become a father figure to him and even the frank, outspoken girl Sophie had befriended the twins. But conditions changed for the worse, nay worst, when Ammu's secret relation with Velutha was revealed. Ammu was tricked into her bedroom and locked.

The twins came there and naturally they wanted to know the reason. Ammu who was not in a mood to weigh her words, had screamed: "If it was not for you I would not be here! None of this would have happened! I would not be here! I would have been free! I should have dumped you in an orphanage the day you were born! You're the millstones round my neck!"[21]

Estha who was sensitive enough and knew what millstones meant, concluded from it that both he and Rahel were unwanted, Ammu did not like them any more. So he decided "that though it was dark and raining, the Time Had Come for them to run away, because Ammu did not want them any more."[22] Estha's plan did not include Sophie but she insisted on joining them and she was able to convince the younger twins to take her with them.[23] Eventually their little boat collided with a floating log and tipped over. Sophie was drowned as she did not know how to swim but the twins survived.[24] All the children had done was intended to arouse the remorse of the elders and win the recognition of their worth. It was also an adventure they hoped to enjoy. It was merely an accident that turned it otherwise. However, Estha was deemed guilty for the death of Sophie. Margaret who slapped him as an immediate response was judicious enough later to write to Ammu to apologise. Unfortunately, others around him were not so kind to him.[25]

Estha, his sister and his mother were allowed to attend the funeral of Sophie Mol but "they were made to stand separately, not with the rest of the family. Nobody would look at them."[26] And then the boy was separated from his mother and sister and returned to his father who hardly loved him. In order to justify the cruelty, a twin expert's opinion was sought and found which declared that there was no harm in separating two-egg twins.[27] It was also argued that the boy needed his father's care and guidance.[28] But what lay behind the camouflage was the bitter truth that Chacko wanted to get rid of his burden and Estha was deemed the worse of the twins. However, the idea to 'return' him to his father originated in the jealous mind of Baby Kochamma.[29]

Estha had to pass through other ordeals before he was 'returned.' Baby Kochamma took him to the Kottayam police station and tricked him into identifying Velutha as the man responsible for kidnapping and murder. Velutha was so dear to him, a father figure and the accusation was false to the core. Still, Estha had to concede to the demands of Baby Kochamma as he thought there was no other way to save his mother.[30]

The experience left a deep, lasting impression on the boy's mind. He "carried inside him the memory of a young man with an old man's mouth. The memory of a swollen face and a smashed, upside down smile...of a bloodshot eye that had opened, wandered and then fixed its gaze on him. Estha. And what had Estha done? He had looked into that beloved face and said: yes."[31] The betrayal leaves a sense of guilt deep in his psyche tormenting him like an 'octopus,' 'like a mango hair between molars.'[32]

Estha had also the sad memory of how Inspector Thomas Mathew misbehaved with his mother and called her 'Veshya.' Though he could not understand what the word meant at the time, the misbehaviour and Ammu's reaction to it had left him uneasy for ever.[33]

Then the most traumatic of his experiences was the one at 'Abhilash Talkies,' a case of sexual abuse by softdrink-seller at the refreshment counter: It created a permanent sense of defilement and a constant apprehension of the return of the man.[34] He always feared that if his mother came to know of it she would begin to love him less.

Returned to his father, much against his wishes, he finished his school with mediocre results without participating in group activities. Then instead of going to the college, he began to do the house work like sweeping, swabbing, laundry, cooking and shopping for vegetables. If he needed anything at meal time, he got up and found it himself. Gradually he stopped talking. The development was not sudden and Estha was a quiet child from the very beginning, so nobody could say exactly when the change took place. It was "the psychological equivalent of what lungfish do to get them through the dry season, except that in Estha's case the dry season looked as though it would lost for ever."[35] He nursed his dog Khubchand well during illness and started walking alone for hours after its death, a habit that stayed with him even when he was 're-returned' to Ayemenem after twenty-three years by his father.[36]

The story of Estha's life raises naturally the question: why is it that he lost his speech? The answer lies in the fact that the boy was brutalised by numerous persons like Baby Kochamma, Kochu Maria, Inspector Mathews and the soft-drink man. Yet neither his disposition nor his circumstances permitted him to protest, to rebel against his tormentors. He had no option but to suffer passively. The voice he could not raise against the injustice done to himself and his dear ones seemed to have lost its utility. That is I think the first reason of his numbness.

The second explanation lies in the sense of shame and guilt that kept him uneasy all the time. The sexual abuse at the refreshment counter, the death of Sophie Mol for which he was accused, the betrayal of Velutha and his end are the contributing factors. An acute feeling of loss, irreparable loss accompanies that sense of shame and guilt and turns his thoughts unspeakable. The boy who had lost all his dear ones and could not find any solace, far less warmth in the company of his father and step mother, had little to express. Discarded by human beings around him, the only comfort his mind could have was in his pet dog Khubchand. Naturally he withdrew himself from the world after the death of Khubchand.

Thirdly, Estha's silence can be explained as a defence mechanism of his agonised soul. There were at least two occasions in his life when speech led to bitter experiences. Had he not started singing in the hall, the sexual abuse at the refreshment counter of the Abhilash Talkies would have never happened.[37] Then, persuaded by Baby Kochamma he said 'yes' to the question of the inspector which meant identifying Velutha as the person guilty for kidnapping and murder. The novelist's immediate observation is: 'Silence slid in like a bolt.'[38]

Estha was a harmless child and so quiet that he was hardly noticed by people around him.[39] "He was the Keeper of Records. The natural custodian of bus tickets, bank receipts, cashmemos, cheque book stubs."[40] Even Baby Kochamma who maligned him so much, found him 'practical,' 'tractable,' 'far sighted' and 'responsible.'[41] That such an innocent child was subjected to the worst cruelty of the adults and his childhood was destroyed and his life ruined for no fault of his own, constitutes a major tragedy in the novel. Such wanton destruction of childhood is staggering to our imagination and pathetic to our heart. "Estha occupied very little space in the world"[42]—and he is also referred to as a "little man."[43] Indeed, he was but a "small thing" thrown back and forth like a ball by elders and their brutality doomed him totally.

Rahel is the younger one of the dizygotic twins because she is younger than her brother Estha by eighteen minutes. The two children share certain common traits as well as they reveal astounding dissimilarities. The similarities we find are the characteristics generally we expect in children while their differences are either representative of a type or can be defined only as their peculiarities.

Innocence is a general trait of childhood and the mind of a child does not function exactly as that of an adult. So both of them think "if they'd been born on the bus, they'd have got free bus rides for the rest of their lives."[44] They also hold that zebra crossings are meant for free funerals and whoever died there, would get it.[45] In the same vein she believes that Sophie Mol "died because she couldn't breathe. Her funeral killed her."[46] When Chacko compares history to an old house at night where the ancestors are whispering, she believes that he was referring to Kari Saipu's house (generally referred to as the 'History House' in the novel).[47] The most remarkable common trait of the twins is their separate but joint identity. They think "of themselves together as Me, and separately, individually, as We or Us."[48]

But Estha and Rahel have got dissimilarities too. Physically they do not "look much like each other."[49] But they differ more profoundly in their mental set-up. While Estha is a timid, polite and quiet boy, a passive sufferer, Rahel is mentally strong, independent and rebellious. She seems to belie the myth that a woman is born weak physically and mentally and cannot but submit to powers that be.

Rahel too has a sad childhood as she had to witness the ill-temper of his alcoholic father in her infancy and had to leave his house for ever when the parents got divorced. She, along with his brother Estha and mother Ammu, had no option but to live at her maternal uncle's house. Soon she came to know that they were unwanted there because Baby Kochamma, Kochu Maria and even Chacko did not hesitate to let them know it. Starved of love as she is even a casual handshake of her mother and maternal uncle is a moment to the twins "treasured and threaded like precious beads on a (somewhat scanty) necklace."[50] For the same reason she asks Chacko if it is possible that Ammu can love Sophie Mol more than her and Estha and Chacko love her more than Sophie Mol.[51]

Deprived as she is of parental love, her mother is both father and mother to her.[52] Then Rahel derives comfort in the company of her brother Estha and together they indulge in plays like reading backwards. That too is a pleasure that Baby Kochamma and Kochu Maria feel jealous for.[53] Finally, Velutha is a lather figure to her. She knows his back as she has been carried on it.[54]

Rahel becomes aware at a tender age that Baby Kochamma and Kochu Maria do not like her. In case of Kochu Maria, she does not hesitate to express her anger in words like ugly, stupid and dwarf.[55] In case of Baby Kochamma, it takes a subtle form. Thus, while attending the funeral of Sophie Mol, she notices a baby bat disturbing Baby Kochamma and she identifies herself with it.[56] Earlier she notices that while everybody pays so much attention to receive Sophie Mol, nobody says hello to her.[57] Her suppressed resentment of elders manifests itself in an apparently senseless mayhem of ants.[58] She has also got a feeling of uncertainty, a fear of insecurity that disrupts the joys of childhood. That is why while attending the funeral of Sophie Mol, she thinks about the sad plight of the painter of the high dome of the church if the rope snapped.[59]

At the tender age of seven, Rahel witnesses and bears the brunt of several tragedies. First when her mother Ammu's secret relation with Velutha is revealed and she is locked in her bedroom, the twins approach to find out the reason. Ammu gives them a reply which shocks the bewildered twins as they do not expect to be called "millstones round my neck" by her.[60] They plan to escape in a boat and as Sophie Mol joins them, one more tragedy occurs as Sophie Mol is drowned accidentally.[61] Then the police arrest and kill Velutha and Rahel has to go to the police station with Estha to identify Velutha as a criminal. They know it well that Velutha is innocent but Baby Kochamma persuades them to do that as the only means to save Ammu.[62]

Baby Kochamma, Chacko and others do not permit Ammu and her children to stand together with them, they have to stand separately. Thus the children are punished for the supposed crime of their mother.[63] But the worst follows the funeral. Four days after the funeral, Chacko batters down the door of the bedroom where Ammu has locked in herself and shouts: 'Get out of my house before I break every bone in your body!' It is so traumatic, so shocking to Rahel that for years she dreams a recurrent dream: "a fat man, faceless, kneeling beside a woman's corpse. Hacking its hair off. Breaking every bone in its body..."[64] Ammu has to leave Ayemenem and dies shortly in a cheap lodge. Powers that be are not merciful to her. Church does not permit to bury her and therefore Chacko covers her with a dirty cloth and gets her cremated.[65] Then her brother Estha too is separated from her as he is sent back to his father.[66] For the rest of her childhood, Rahel is denied the privilege of even seeing his brother as he is returned again to Ayemenem after no less than twenty-three years. One can imagine how woeful the childhood of Rahel has become. As the novelist puts it: "While other children of their age learned other things, Estha and Rahel learned how history negotiates its terms and collects its dues from those who break its laws."[67]

We have also to take note of her experiences at school to complete the picture of her childhood. She drifts from school to school after the death of her mother and spends her holidays in Ayemenem. She is largely ignored by Chacko and Mammachi and largely ignores Baby Kochamma. Chacko and Mammachi provide her care (food, clothes, fees) but they have withdrawn concern. Strangely enough, the neglect in her case results in an "accidental release of the spirit."[68]

The teachers of the schools she attends find her "extremely polite" but having "no friends." However, the heads of the institutions are not satisfied with her behaviour. The incidents mentioned in the novel reveal the problems of adolescence as well as the senseless and hypocritical attitude of the heads of the institutions. First, she is caught outside her Headmistress' garden gate decorating a knob of fresh cowdung with small flowers. The eleven year old girl is condemned for depravity the next morning at Assembly. Now, we learn from a well-informed critic Pramod K. Nayar that such decoration is related to Onam festival.[69] Under the circumstances, the Headmistress' behaviour shows either her utter ignorance of or total disregard for the culture of Kerala. Six months later, Rahel is expelled from Nazareth Convent after repeated complaints from senior girls.

She is accused of hiding behind doors and deliberately colliding with her seniors. Cajoled, caned and starved, she admits having "done it to find out whether breasts hurt." As breasts are not supposed even to exist in a Christian institution, Rahel is expelled. A sane principal should have realised that such curiosity is not quite unusual at that age and no girl need be expelled for it.

Rahel is expelled from the second school for smoking. That is also characteristic of an adolescent's curious nature. Many children of that age try to find out why their elders smoke and how pleasant or otherwise it is. Strangely enough, smoking in case of boys is overlooked if not encouraged at home and school but condemned as a heinous crime in case of girls. Rahel's expulsion is a typical instance of this hypocrisy.

Rahel's third expulsion is "for setting fire to her Headmistress' false hair bun which, under duress, Rahel confessed to have stolen."[70] Here we find her protesting in an unusual way against artificiality.

Thus, Rahel shows a strong personality. Though circumstances are hardly favourable to her, they fail to break her will and spirit. She is a rebel who faces all odds and survives to help her brother Estha when he is 're-returned' twenty-three years later.

Now, we are in a position to say what the novelist thinks about the plight of children in India. The first thing that strikes us is the insensitivity of Indian adults to the psychology of the children. Even the educated fail miserably in this respect. Sophie Mol's guardians do not care to see that she needs the company of children. Attempts are made by them to keep her aloof and she befriends Estha and Rahel on her own. The twins are scolded for things which cannot but be called innocent play. Not satisfied with that elders teach them how to pretend, to lie and to betray. Even the best among the adults fail to bridge the gap between themselves and the children. Ammu never comes to know that her son was a victim of child abuse. She does not even suspect it. Estha dares not tell it to his mother, though he discloses it to his sister. Such communication gaps permit the culprits to escape scot free. Despite all the rhetoric, children are neglected in our society and little care is taken to understand them and provide them the attention and security they need. Even when laws are enacted to protect them, they are seldom enforced because the guardians are insensitive and the politicians need not bother about children as they are simply non-entities in electoral politics.

REFERENCES

1. Ministry of Labour, *Annual Report 1983-84* (GOI, New Delhi, 1985), 54.
2. Weiner, Myron, *The Child and the State in India*, Princeton University Press, 1991, 78.
3. *Ibid.*, 20-21.
4. *Ibid.*, 43.
5. Naik, J.P., *Elementary Education in India: A Promise to Keep*, Bombay, 1975, 10.
6. Weiner, Myron, *op. cit.*, 205-207.
7. Milligan, James, M.D., *Violence: Reflections on a National Epidemic*, New York, 1996, 192.
8. *Ibid.*, 196.
9. Roy, Arundhati, *The God of Small Things*, London, 1998, 42.
10. *Ibid.*, 43.
11. *Ibid.*, 45.
12. *Ibid.*, 57.
13. *Ibid.*, 85-86.
14. *Ibid.*, 83.
15. *Ibid.*, 36.
16. *Ibid.*, 157.
17. *Ibid.*, 46.
18. *Ibid.*, 60.
19. *Ibid.*, 149.

20. Roy, Arundhati, *The God of Small Things,* London, 1998, 151.
21. *Ibid.*, 253.
22. *Ibid.*, 264.
23. *Ibid.*, 292.
24. *Ibid.*, 292-293.
25. *Ibid.*, 264.
26. *Ibid.*, 6.
27. *Ibid.*, 32.
28. *Ibid.*, 31.
29. *Ibid.*, 322, 31.
30. *Ibid.*, 318.
31. *Ibid.*, 32.
32. *Ibid.*
33. *Ibid.*, 7-8.
34. *Ibid.*, 194, 197.
35. *Ibid.*, 10.
36. *Ibid.*, 12-13.
37. *Ibid.*, 100-103.
38. *Ibid.*, 320.
39. *Ibid.*, 10.
40. *Ibid.*, 163.
41. *Ibid.*, 319.
42. *Ibid.*, 11.
43. *Ibid.*, 319.
44. *Ibid.*, 3-4.
45. *Ibid.*, 4.
46. *Ibid.*, 7.
47. *Ibid.*, 52-53.
48. *Ibid.*, 2.
49. *Ibid.*
50. *Ibid.*, 62.
51. *Ibid.*, 118.
52. *Ibid.*, 149.
53. *Ibid.*, 17.
54. *Ibid.*, 73.
55. *Ibid.*, 185.
56. *Ibid.*, 6.
57. *Ibid.*, 173.
58. *Ibid.*, 185-186.

59. Roy, Arundhati, *The God of Small Things*, London, 1998, 6.
60. *Ibid.*, 253.
61. *Ibid.*, 292.
62. *Ibid.*, 310, 311, 319.
63. *Ibid.*, 5.
64. *Ibid.*, 225.
65. *Ibid.*, 159-163.
66. *Ibid.*, 326.
67. *Ibid.*, 55.
68. *Ibid.*, 15-17.
69. Dhawan, R.K., (ed.), *Arundhati Roy The Novelist Extraordinary*, New Delhi, 1999, 238.
70. Roy, Arundhati, *op. cit.* 17.

5

THE DOWNTRODDEN IN THE NOVEL

It is an irony of civilization that people who work hardest to produce riches suffer the most and fare the worst. They are looked down upon and treated shabbily by the powerful. We know them as 'working class,' a term used all over the world. They are included in the "small things" Arundhati Roy speaks for. But Indian tradition has left as a legacy of the Aryan past a section which is placed worse than ordinary members of the working class. That is known generally as 'untouchable' or 'pariah.' As it sounds bitter, Mahatma Gandhi named them as 'Harijans' (children of God) while the Census authorities during the British rule referred to them as 'exterior classes.' Nowadays they are popularly known as the 'depressed' or 'dalits.'

There is a lot of ambiguity about the reasons that gave birth to the institution of untouchability and the date of its appearance. Thus, we learn from Romila Thapar that untouchability derived from the fact that some people were "considered polluting either because of their occupation as scavengers, such as Candalas and Doms and those who maintained the cremation grounds, or because they belonged to primitive tribes such as the Nisada and Bhilla. Their speech was alien and their manner of life was strange. Even the Buddhists despised of the Candalas. The inequities of city life further aggravated the degradation of these groups, already declared impure on account of ritual pollution."[1]

R.S. Sharma thinks that untouchability is a phenomenon that developed sometime before the Mauryas. As for the causes, he puts them briefly as follows: "Against the background of a very low material culture of the aborigines, the increasing contempt for manual work, combined with primitive ideas of taboo and impurity associated with certain materials, produced the unique phenomenon of untouchability. This was particularly true of the work of the Candalas who dealt with corpses, with which were linked the primitive ideas of impurity and horror. Consequently it was felt necessary to avoid contact with such persons. In later times the idea of untouchability was extended."[2]

According to Prabhati Mukherjee, untouchability was the punishment the forest-dwelling rebels got for their insubordination and hostility to the Aryas. "When they were brought under subjugation eventually, they were neither incorporated into the main economic activity prevailing at that time, that is, agriculture, nor into any other form of production in society. Only unskilled, unproductive, lowly and menial jobs were assigned to them. Thus, when they were forced to surrender it was not clemency they received. Instead, they were treated with utter contempt and were segregated as a residual category of people to be employed as and when necessary."[3]

Prabhati Mukherjee seems to base her contention on the much publicised theory of the Aryan invasion of India. Foreign conquerors of a fair-skinned race according to the adherents of the theory subjugated the dark-skinned aborigines and placed them at the lower levels of society with the result that part of them became the fourth class of society and part of them, untouchables. The trouble with this theory is that the Aryan invasion of India is no longer as undisputed as it was in the nineteenth century. A number of scholars (both Indian and foreign), challenge the theory now. Thus, Colin Renfrew observes: "When Wheeler speaks of 'the Aryan invasion of the Land of the Seven Rivers, the Punjab,' he has no warranty at all, so far as I can see. If one checks the dozen references in the *Rigveda* to the Seven Rivers, there is nothing in any of them that to me implies invasion: the land of the Seven Rivers is the land of the *Rigveda,* the scene of action. Nothing implies that the Aryas were strangers there. Nor is it implied that the inhabitants of the walled cities (including the Dasyus) were any more aboriginal than the Aryas themselves."[4] J.G. Shaffer declares: "Current archaeological data do not support the existence of an Indo-European or European invasion into South Asia at any time in the pre- or proto-historic periods. Instead, it is possible to document archaeologically a series of cultural changes reflecting indigenous cultural development from pre-historic to historic periods."[5] Indian scholars like Bhagwan Singh, K.D. Sethna and S.G. Talageri are only a few of the challengers to the theory of invasion.[6] Finally, even if we admit the theory of Aryan invasion, it fails to explain why a section of the aborigines became untouchables while the rest became the fourth varna. The hostility lasting for centuries itself demands explanation which is not forthcoming.

Dr. B.R. Ambedkar does not believe in the Aryan conquest of India.[7] He has examined Stanley Rice's theory that the pre-Dravidian aborigines were made untouchables by the Dravidians and the latter were made the Shudras by the Aryan conquerors. He quotes a lot of anthropometric data and sums up as follows: "If anthropometry is a science which can be depended upon to determine the race of a people, then the result obtained by the application of anthropometry to the various strata of Hindu society disprove that the untouchables belong to a race different from the Aryans and Dravidians. The measurements establish that the Brahmins and the Untouchables belong to the same race. From this it follows that if the Brahmins are Aryans the Untouchables are also Aryans. If the Brahmins are Dravidians the Untouchables are also Dravidians."[8]

Ambedkar contends that when tribes began to settle on land and started agricultural activities, all of them did not settle simultaneously. So there were frequent clashes between settled and nomadic tribes with the result that a section of the nomadic tribes were broken. The Broken Men could not be integrated and had to stay on the outskirts of the villages. They became Buddhists in course of time. Contempt for Buddhism reduced these Broken Men to untouchables later. As these Broken Men used to eat the flesh of the dead cows, that became another factor contributing to the evolution of untouchability. Ambedkar believes that "Untouchability was born some time around 4th century A.D."[9]

U.N. Roy in his 'Origin of Untouchability' has examined the views of Dr. Ambedkar at length. He disagrees with Ambedkar about the date as well as the roots of untouchability.[10] As to the date, he has shown that untouchability was practised long before the fourth century and Panini, Kautilya and Buddha were well acquainted with it.[11] As to the roots of untouchability, he holds that it is a product of the conflict between food-gathering and food-producing people. The former were feared for certain practices like stealing women, children and cattle and customs like human sacrifice. They were also hated by settled people as they took food which was tabooed by the settled (like flesh of dead animals and dogs). They could not be integrated into the settled communities and had to stay apart. The real reasons of keeping them apart were forgotten later and they became untouchables as people are more afraid of the unknown than of the known.

It is generally believed that there were no untouchables in the Vedic age and they were merely a later addition to Indian society which had four varnas only. This view has resulted in the currency of a new word, 'pancham' (the fifth class) for the untouchables. Sanskrit scholars find it difficult to subscribe to this view because grammarians like Panini and Patanjali called the untouchables like Chandal and Mritapa the 'excluded shudras' (Nirvasit Shudras) and law makers called them 'asat shudras.'[12] Obviously, then, they were not intended to be placed outside the society but treated as a section of the Shudra varna which constituted the fourth class of Indian society. So a word like 'pancham' must have come into being during the days when Sanskrit texts were either forgotten or misunderstood.

The untouchables have been subjected to several social disabilities. They were not permitted to live in and enter into settlements but for specific purposes and limited span of time. People of other caste could use vessels touched by them and avoided their contact. They had to reside at the outskirts of the villages and towns and could not enter unannounced.

The circular letter issued by the Census Commissioner in 1910 laid down five criteria to ascertain the identity of the untouchables. As they describe the disabilities they faced, it is worthwhile to quote them:

- Do not receive the Mantra from a Brahman or other recognized Hindu guru.
- Are not served by good Brahmanas as family priests.
- Have no Brahman priests at all.
- Are denied access to the interior of the Hindu temples.
- Eat beef and do no reverence to the cow.

Dr. Mutton has given his own criteria which shed more light on the condition of the untouchables:

- Do not receive the services of the Brahmanas, Ksatriyas and Vaishyas.
- Are not served by barbers and kahars (water-carrier and palanquin bearing caste).
- Cannot serve food and water to higher castes.
- Cannot enter into temples, holy places etc.
- Cannot use wells, ponds, roads, hotels etc. meant for public use.
- Cannot give up filthy occupations and adopt other ones.

Kshitimohan Sen mentions five categories of the untouchables: "The water touched by a low caste is not accepted. Lower are the people who pollute earthen ware by their touch. Lower than them are people who pollute even the metal vessels by their touch. Lower even than them are the castes who pollute a temple by entering into the yard. There are even castes who pollute the entire village or town they enter."[13]

Untouchability was practised more rigorously in South India than elsewhere. Brahmanas and other 'higher' castes believed themselves to become polluted if Kammalan (blacksmiths, carpenters etc.) approached within sixteen hands, toddy trappers within twenty-four, Pollaya or Cheruma (peasants) within thirty-two and Paria within forty hands. Nayadi were kept at a distance of more than two hundred hands. Tanks of higher castes became unworthy of use if the untouchables passed by them. Untouchables could not wear gold ornaments, nor use umbrellas and foot-wear. They could not attend schools where children of other castes were enrolled. In Maharashtra, they had to drag a thorny branch to wipe out their footprints and had to be prostrate themselves at a distance when a Brahmana passed by so that their shadow might not defile the Brahmana. In Kerala, untouchability assumed its most appalling features. "It is no wonder that the land looked like a lunatic asylum to Vivekanand when he first visited Kerala."[14]

Protests against untouchability were heard first in a religious form during the middle ages. They neither aimed exclusively at eradicating untouchability nor were they aggressive. Yet they had some impact on society. Some of the religious figures of the times were themselves untouchables. Raidas, for example was born a cobbler. Nabhadas was a Dom. Kabir, Nanak, Dadu and Sri Chaitanyadev were not untouchables but their liberal teachings contributed a lot to ameliorate the lot of the downtrodden. In Kerala too, Veer Kerala Verma, the seventeenth century soldier-litterateur argued for the equality of the Brahmana and the Pariah because they did not differ in birth, hunger, suffering and feeling. "The dying is alike and the corpses carry out no distinction."[15]

The nineteenth century witnessed the rise of some socio-religious movements which questioned the rigours of caste-system and untouchability. Brahma Samaj in Bengal, Prarthana Samaj and Satyashodhak Samaj in Maharashtra and Arya Samaj in Punjab appealed for a better attitude toward the lowest sections of society on spiritual grounds. A similar approach to social questions was adopted by Chattapi Swami (1854-1924), Shri Narayan Guru (died 1928) and Swami Agamananda (1896-1961) in Kerala. The first two of them belonged to the untouchable Ezhava community. Shri Narayan Guru, known as "the Great Guru" was the author of two works in Tamil, eight in Sanskrit and over thirty in Malayalam. "He rejected the distinctions of caste and religion which divided men and fought all through his life for a unity based on equality, mutual reverence and love."[16]

Shri Narayan Guru had a disciple in the poet Kumaran Asan (1873-1924), who handled an old Buddhist legend in a fluent, musical narration. The problem of untouchability caught the imagination of the well-known poet Vallathol (1878-1958) too. One of his poems tells the story of a high-caste patriarch whose mansion catches fire. A so-called untouchable is about to draw water from the well to put out the fire. But the old man would rather see the house burnt down than bear the thought of his well being polluted.

Social disabilities suffered by the untouchables received a nationwide attention as two great personalities of India dedicated themselves to the cause of untouchables. Dr. B.R. Ambedkar, himself a Mahar (an untouchable caste of Maharashtra) organised untouchables and agitated for them to the end of his life in 1956. He had his differences with Mahatina Gandhi and other nationalist leaders but that did not hinder the acceptance of the cause of untouchables as a cause of the nation. Mahatma Gandhi, impressed by the importance of their problems founded Harijan Sevak Sangha headed by Thakkar Bapa. In 1934, he gave up even ordinary membership of Indian National Congress to devote his time and energy exclusively to the cause of untouchables. He wrote regularly for the *Harijan,* the organ of Harijan Sevak Sangha. The 'ashramas' set up by Mahatma Gandhi and his disciples made no distinction between the touchables and untouchables and his example led others in the national movement to renounce the traditional outlook and behaviour.

Social action in Kerala for the Ezhavas found an organizational expression in Shri Narayana Dharma Paripalana Yogam (SNDPY) inspired by the teachings of Shri Narayana Guru. Ayyan Kali (1866-1961) created a similar organization for the Palaya community whose disabilities were greater than those of the Ezhavas. Two journalists belonging to the Ezhava community, C. Krishnan (1867-1935) and T.K. Madhavan (1886-1930) editors of *Mitavadi* and *Deshabhimani,* respectively played an important role in the struggle for social reform.. The movement gained the first major victory when approach roads to the great temple at Vaikom were opened to all castes in 1925. Approach roads to all temples in Travancore were opened to all by 1928. A similar demand in case of Guru Vayur (1931-32) did not end in immediate success but had a positive effect in moulding public opinion. The ruler of Travancore issued Temple Entry Proclamation on November

12, 1936 removing all restrictions to the entry based on caste. The ruler of Cochin followed suit with a similar proclamation in 1947-48. Earlier Shri Narayan Guru had consecrated temples for the Ezhava community with Ezhava priests as the Ezhavas were not permitted to worship in the shrines of higher castes. Now the Devaswam Board of Kerala trains and appoints priests from all Hindu communities, including the so-called untouchables.[17]

V.V. Kukikrishan's essay 'Communists and their social activities in Malabar' shows that the Communist Party played a role in awakening the untouchables. As Vinita Bhatnagar sums up their activities: "Schools and reading rooms were established. Mass education programmes were launched which attempted to create a cultural change among the illiterate and impoverished people."[18]

The *Constitution* of India which came into force with effect from January 26, 1950 was drafted by the well-known leader of the untouchables, Dr. B.R. Ambedkar. It gave right to equality to all citizens of India under Articles 14, 15 and 16. But most remarkable of all was the assurance given in Article 17:

> "Untouchability" is abolished and its practice in any form is forbidden. The enforcement of any disability arising out of "untouchability" shall be an offence punishable in accordance with law.

The "untouchables" listed in a schedule and therefore known as scheduled castes are now granted guaranteed admissions to schools and colleges (including medical and engineering colleges), a percentage of central and state government jobs is reserved for them and as a number of constituencies are reserved for them, they are guaranteed representation in Parliament and state assemblies too.

That seems to be a positive development but we need not conclude from the above that everything is okay for the dalits. Even Shashi Tharoor who draws a rosy picture otherwise has to concede the following in his book *India from Midnight to the Millennium*: "Despite fifty years of freedom, well-trained and enlightened administrators, and politically correct rhetoric at all levels, caste continues to enslave village society. Each week brings a new horror story into the national press. A dalit woman is stripped and paraded naked through the streets of her village because her son dared to steal from an upper-caste Thakur; she is then forced to have sex with the offending boy before a sneering audience of Thakurs. A high born Jat girl falls in love with an untouchable boy and is caught trying to elope with him; they and their accomplice, another untouchable are caught, beaten, tortured in front of their families, and hanged, and their bodies are then burned (the girl is not immediately killed by her noose, and is still alive when the fire is lit; she tries to crawl out, but is thrown back into the flames). In one village, twenty-two 'uppity' untouchables are gunned down in an upper-caste massacre; in another, four hundred dalit families are burned out of their huts for daring to demand the legal minimum wage for their labours. These are not isolated incidents, in that dozens like them are reported every year."[19]

Such incidents represent resistance to change no doubt but not the impossibility of it. Shashi Tharoor finds the condition of the untouchables in Kerala better than that in other parts of India. "A combination of enlightened rule by the far-thinking maharajahs, progressive reform movements within the Hindu tradition (especially that of remarkable Ezhava, sage Shri Narayan Guru), and changes wrought by a series of left-dominated legislature since independence have given Kerala's Scheduled Castes a place in society that other Dalits (former untouchables) across India are still denied."[20]

Arundhati Roy's presentation of the dalits has provoked a lot of controversy. She is often accused of drawing a gloomy picture of the dalits which is related to their past rather than present in Kerala. It is also said that she has underplayed the role of the Communists for the uplift of the dalits in Kerala. For sake of brevity we have to observe that the militant image of a party does not remain unchanged when it comes to power. A party in power becomes more and more concerned with retaining power and concedes more and more to the prejudices that prevail for appeasing the electorate. That is what Arundhati seeks to make out in the novel. As to the existence of the prejudices in Kerala, even today, we find a positive proof in Abu Abraham's article, "Breaking the Love Laws" published in *The Hindustan Times Sunday Magazine*,

November, 23, 1997, P.3. Abu Abraham takes Arundhati Roy to task for denigrating E.M.S. Namboodripad and CPI (M) and proceeds to declare it "clearly obscene" that "a Syrian Christian woman would make love to an untouchable youth." What would such "progressives" say about Sarojini's marriage with a Naidu?

The novelist's presentation of the dalits is constantly blended with irony. People well-placed in society attempt to be kind and sympathetic to them but their deep-rooted prejudices and the fear of losing their supremacy undermine their professed liberal or revolutionary aims. A gentleman wants to educate the untouchables but dares not place them in the same school with the touchables. A leader talks about social revolution but dreads an untouchable who holds the party card. An employer recognises the merits of her employee but attaches more importance to his caste.

Then, the untouchable characters in the novel are presented as types. The device proves useful for the purpose of giving a realistic view of the varying responses to the grim reality of the dalits. The fact can not be disputed that though the dalits are subjected to a similar treatment by the upper castes, their responses are not uniform.

We come across three characters in *The God of Small Things* which belong to the category of the downtrodden. They are Vellya Paapen and his two sons Kuttapen and Velutha. They belong to an untouchable caste called Paravan. They are toddy trappers according to the tradition. Arundhali Roy gives a lot of information about the untouchables of Kerala in this connection. She also gives a generally perfect picture of the dalits with their varying responses to the caste oppression through the device of trio. Vellya Paapen, Kuttapen and Velutha constitute the trio which depicts the three types of the dalits in Indian society, namely, the docile conformist, the discontented paralytic and the rebel who moves for equality and stakes his life.

The novel mentions only the names of three untouchable castes, namely, Paravans, Palayas and Pulayas. They were not allowed to enter into the house of Touchables. "Mammachi told Estha and Rahel that she could remember a time, in her girlhood, when Paravans were expected to crawl backwards with a broom, sweeping away their footprints so that Brahmins or Syrian Christians would not defile themselves by accidentally stepping into a Paravan's footprints. In Mammachi's time, Paravans, like other Untouchables, were not allowed to walk on public roads, not allowed to cover their upper bodies, not allowed to carry umbrellas. They had to put their hands over their mouths when they spoke, to divert their polluted breath away from those whom they addressed."[21]

Even earlier than the days of Mammachi's girlhood, there were liberal people who wanted to enlighten these poor fellows. However, they could not even think of a common school for children of all castes. That is why they had to build separate schools for untouchable children. The great grandfather of Estha had done so for them.[22] That seems curious to us as we have heard more about separate schools for girls only.

Conditions have changed since then. They do not have to carry brooms during the childhood of Estha and Rahel. They use public roads. They are also learning skills other than their traditional occupations. Though that does not bring as much monetary gain to them as to the touchable folk. For example, Mammachi pays Velutha more than she normally does to a Paravan but less than that to a touchable.[23] Neither the orthodox Mammachi nor the 'progressive' Pillai permit them to step inside their houses.[24] The untouchables are becoming members of the Communist Party and trade unions and marching along with others in processions wearing shirts.[25] They are introduced to the idea of equal rights but we are also informed that Touchable workers grudge their equal rights. We have reasons to suspect that such backward sentiments are encouraged by well-to-do classes with vested interests even when they masquerade as communists. Chacko and Pillai are instances to the point.[26] Chacko as a factory-owner wants to prevent the growth of real trade union led by Velutha in his factory. Pillai finds a threat to his ambitions in Velutha as the latter's working class background seems a plus point in the race for party and trade union leadership. The presentation of the dalits is ironical as pointed out earlier. Untouchables having become aware of the stigma that is attached to their castes demand now "that untouchables no longer be addressed by their caste names."[27]

It is remarkable to note that the institution of untouchability has not left Christianity unaffected. Even the communists in the pursuit of immediate electoral gains submit to it. So far as Christians in India are concerned, they are but the converts from Hindu Society. They have replaced their faith with the *Bible* and Christ, but retained the mores of their Hindu past. An upper caste Christian is no better than an upper caste Hindu in his social attitude. The prejudices are particularly strong in South India where we find separate cemeteries for untouchables and others. Arundhati Roy does not fail to inform us what Christianity has done to the untouchables in Kerala. Syrian Christians of Kerala are converts from higher castes "by and large, the wealthy, estate-owning feudal lords" who "had always voted for the Congress Party."[28] Christianity did not prove a boon to the untouchables. When the British came to Malabar, some of them converted to Christianity and joined the Anglican Church. Velutha's grandfather, Kelan was one among them. They hoped to escape the scourge of untouchability. They were also given some food and money and so came to be known as "Rice-Christians." They realized soon that "they had jumped from the frying pan into the fire." They got separate churches, separate services, separate priests and even their own separate Pariah Bishop. Because they were deemed casteless as Christians officially, they got no benefits like job reservations or bank loans at low interest rates.[29] To sum up, Christianity has not removed the prejudices and arrogance of the converts from the upper castes, nor ameliorated the lot of the converts from the untouchable communities. It has kept the social hierarchy inherited from the past intact. She seems to imply that conversion is no remedy for people subjected to social discrimination. Secular factors are likely to prove more helpful to them. Mammachi admits Velutha to her house when there is something to mend or to instal and he is admitted to the factory because of his mechanical skills.[30]

Vellya Paapen, the oldest of the three untouchables in the novel is an "Old World Paravan" as the novelist puts it.[31] Born and brought up in the age when Paravans had to crawl backwards, he takes for granted the social disabilities imposed on the untouchables by tradition. He dares not question or violate the caste rules. Obviously he believes that it will be sinful to deviate. That makes him a defender of social status quo, a zealous guardian of conformity, highly fearful of change.

As in his social outlook, so also in his general outlook, he is superstitious by nature. One may argue that his superstition has shaped his social outlook. He believes in ghosts. As Kari Saipu had committed suicide, he holds that he has become a ghost. As he goes across the river one day in search of a nutmeg tree, he smells cigar smoke and whirls around and hurls his sickle at the smell. Thus he loses his sickle but finds a satisfaction in the thought that he has pinned the 'paedophile ghost' to the trunk of a rubber tree and put an end to his wanderings.[32]

With his deep-rooted faith in tradition, Vellya fears for his younger son. He resents his "lack of hesitation," his "unwarranted assurance." He cannot find fault with him in what he says or does but he dislikes his self-assuredness, his confidence. He resents "the way he says, the way he does"[33] Strangely enough, his concern anticipates the complaint of Baby Kochamma to the police: "She described to Inspector Thomas Mathew how it was not just *what* Velutha had said that had made her to come but the way he said it."[34]

The old man fails to explain to Velutha what bothers him and as his son thinks he is grudging his training and natural skills, nagging and bickering begin. So Velutha avoids going home. Then, he disappears from the village for four years. When he returns, his mother Chella has died of tuberculosis. Vellya finds his younger son's manners even more worrying but he keeps quiet to avoid quarrel.[35] He breaks his silence only when the Terror takes hold of him.[36]

Vellya Paapen has a gratitude to Mammachi and her family which is "as wide and deep as a river in spate."[37] They have done so much for his family for generations. Reverend E. John Ipe gave Vellya's father, Kelan, title to the land on which his hut now stands.[38] Then, when Vellya had an accident and lost one of his eyes, Mammachi paid for his glass eye.[39] Of course, it was paid as a loan but Vellya has not been able to work off his debt nor seems to be able to do that ever. He is also grateful to Mammachi for she arranged Velutha's education and gave him a job.[40] That Mammachi and her family too have benefited from their labour does not occur to him.

So when he comes to know of what his son has done, he feels obliged to go to Mammachi to report. He weeps and trembles and offers to return his mortgaged eye. He asks "God's forgiveness for having spawned a monster" and offers "to kill his son with his own bare hands."[41] This is because his son and Mammachi's...daughter have "made the unthinkable thinkable and the impossible really happen."[42] As they go to Kari Saipu's house to meet, Vellya Paapen believes that Kari Saipu's demon has entered them, it is "Kari Saipu's revenge for what he, Vellya Paapen, had done to him." Mammachi does not at first believe him and pushes him with all her strength. He falls down and lies "sprawled in the wet mud" while she continues calling him names like 'drunken dog' and 'drunken Paravan liar.'[43] It is only Baby Kochamma who takes it as credible.

Thus it is Vellya Paapen's feelings like gratitude and loyalty that prompt him to disclose what he has seen and learned to Mammachi instead of warning his son first. That hastens the doom of Velutha. In the conflict between 'loyalty' and 'love' the former gains the upper hand. As the novelist remarks: "By the time he understood his part in History's Plans, it was too late to retrace his steps. He had swept his footprints away himself. Crawling backwards with a broom."[44]

Ranjana Harish contrasts Vellya Paapen with his younger son Velutha in terms of symbols of 'mombatti' and mirror. Mombattis (candles) stand for "smallness as well as of illumination. Smallness of small people is fine but their being self-illuminated is something which cannot be taken by the establishment. All small men are not 'Mombattis,' most of them usually are pieces of mirror reflecting Laltain Sahib's light."[45] While Velutha is a Mombatti whose life is "guided by inner light and not by the laws of the society." Vellya Paapen is a mirror reflecting the light of Mammachi and Baby Kochamma.[46] Thus he symbolises the docile, conformist section of the dalits.

Kuttapen is the elder son of Vellya Paapen. He lives in a little laterite hut down river from the Ayemenem House with his father and younger brother.[47] He is not educated and pursues traditional jobs of his caste until he becomes disabled. That happens when he falls off a coconut tree and his spine is damaged. He has become paralysed and unable to work since then.[48] While his father and younger brother go to work, he lies flat on his back. A black hen in the hut is the only company he has. Paralysed from chest downwards, he has lost sensation in his feet and cannot use them. He keeps a stick to defend himself against snakes.[49] For his requirements like water to drink and towel to wipe the grit off his face and neck he depends on others, mostly his brother.[50] In fact, Kuttapen's physical immobility might be interpreted as being symbolic of his mental state. Unlike his younger brother he has not moved forward with the times and grasped no progressive ideas. His paralysis in body corresponds to his immobility of mind, that is, his fear of the new, his fear of progress.

He is polite to Estha and Rahel when they visit him. He is curious about Sophie Mol and tells them that generally speaking, it is not difficult to mend a boat—but warns them about its use.[51] He is aware of the trade union and political activities of his younger brother and seems to be worried about its consequences.[52]

As he lies on his hard bed, bits of thatch and grit fall from the ceiling and mingle with his sweat. Sometimes ants and insects fall with it. Bored with the life of insignificance he is living, he envies mad men who can walk and seems willing to barter his sanity for "serviceable legs."[53] This longing for insanity symbolises his dissatisfaction with the stasis. Though he is unable to move, he hates to be immobile. But to move in case of a Paravan means to move beyond the limits imposed by society, to transgress its laws which amounts to madness and annihilation as in the case of Velutha. Kuttapen is well aware of the fact that society deals heavily with transgressors and dares not "move" fearing the consequences.

Kuttapen remembers how his mother Chella suffered and died and misses her much. Lying on his bed, he coughs like his mother and the upper part of his body bucks "like a just-caught fish." In the small hut he shares with his father and brother, one corner is reserved for cooking, one for clothes, one for bedding-rolls. That leaves the other corner where his mother died. That corner he has chosen for himself as he believes it is reserved for dying in.[54]

Kuttapen is "a good, safe Paravan" because he cannot read or write. That is, though there are schools for untouchables, people in power prefer to keep them illiterate because that is less likely to awaken their social consciousness. Ignorant people are less able to protest and defy than the awakened. Being close to the generation of his father and devoid of progressive ideas, he poses no threat to the well-placed in society.

Having lost all his interest in life, he whiles his time by singing a Malayalam song time and again and waits for death. He assumes, not without reason, that he, will the first in the family to "follow in his mother's wake." Soon he learns he was wrong. Velutha is murdered brutally by the police which leaves his unfortunate bròther even more paralysed than ever.

Velutha, the younger son of Vellya Paapen is not a conformist like his father and elder brother. He is not a mirror which reflects the image of the dominating section of the society. He is not and cannot become a "Laltain" needing oil from outside as he does not belong to the class of exploiters. He is a 'Mombatti' (candle) burning by himself. He is self-illumined and self-confident and has got the self-esteem—the qualities which make a man remarkable.

These are the very qualities that frighten his father. His father is fearful because such qualities in a Paravan are not appreciated. "While these qualities were perfectly acceptable, perhaps even desirable in Touchables, Vellya Paapen thought that in a Paravan they could (and would, and indeed, *should*) be construed as insolence."[55]

Velutha's name is rather ironical because the word means 'white' in Malayalam but his complexion is black. This conflict between the name and reality seems to be indicative of other conflicts in the novel of the same type. As M. Dasan remarks in his essay "Arundhati Hits the Social-Political Ball": "Velutha is placed on the borders of society, caught in between right and wrong; sanity and insanity; morality and immorality. This untouchable master craftsman floats on the periphery of society yearning to be accepted, confided and recognised like O'Neil's Black protagonist, Yank, in *The Hairy Ape.*"[56]

Velutha is about three years younger than Ammu. He is not illiterate like his father and elder brother because when he was about eleven, Mammachi noticed his natural skills and persuaded his father to send him to the Untouchable's school founded by her father-in-law, Punyan Kunju. Besides he has got natural skills to prepare intricate toys with dried palm reeds, tapioca stems and cashew nuts. He has learned carpentry from a German carpenter, Johann Klein and knows a lot about machines. "Mammachi (with impenetrable Touchable logic) often said that if only he hadn't been a Paravan, he might have become an engineer." As a matter of fact, Velutha has served Mammachi and Chacko well both at their house and at the factory with his various skills. So he deserves the praise.[57] It is ironical, however, that his remuneration does not correspond to this praise and his abilities are not duly rewarded. To his employers and even to his party leaders, he remains only a Paravan.

But his "lack of hesitation" and "unwarranted assurance" annoy his father, a Paravan of old days. The old attempts to warn his son disturb the peace at home and Velutha avoids going home at first and then disappears. He remains incognito for four years and returns one year after the death of his mother. Nobody knows for sure where he has been during the period and what he has done. There are rumours of different types about him because even after his return, he has not disclosed his whereabouts.[58]

Velutha has been working as a factory carpenter before his sudden disappearance. Mammachi rehired him after his return and put him in charge of general maintenance. That did not please the Touchable factory workers. Mammachi puts that situation to a profitable use by paying "Velutha less than she would to a Touchable carpenter but more than she would a Paravan."[59] He is allowed to enter the house of Mammachi to mend or instal something only and she thinks he ought to be grateful that he is allowed on the factory premises and permitted to touch things that Touchables touch.[60]

Though we are not sure of the four years mentioned above, soon after his return to Ayemenem we find him marching with a red flag in his hand and a white shirt on his body in a procession led by the Travancore-Cochin Marxist Labour Union. He is recognised by Rahel, though Ammu and Estha do not want to admit that in presence of Baby Kochamma and Chacko for obvious reasons. The event seems to be a minor one but proves so significant in reality.[61]

Baby Kochamma is humiliated by the processionists and when she hears the name of Velutha mentioned in connection with the procession, she finds an easy target for her wrath which is transferred against Velutha. Even though Rahel is not sure about his presence and Estha expresses strong doubts about it, Baby Kochamma discovers "some rudeness, some ingratitude in Velutha's behaviour and waits for an opportunity to victimize him. Chacko too shows much concern about it."[62] Though he does not think it likely because Velutha is "a Paravan with a future." He wonders whether Velutha has "become a card-holding member of the Marxist Party and has been seeing Comrade K.N.M. Pillai lately."[63]

The procession leaves its mark on the two children Estha and Rahel too. Rahel knows his back well because she has been carried on it. It has a light brown birthmark shaped like a pointed dry leaf, a leaf he deems lucky.[64] But for the shirt he has put on, Rahel feels sure about his identity. She watches him carrying a red flag in his hand and feels excited about it. "The flag had seemed to her a most impressive piece of equipment. The right thing for a friend to have."[65] Rahel visits Velutha the next days and tells him what she has seen. At first Velutha tries to deny it with not so serious excuses and then has "a lovely laugh."[66] Thereafter the two children become fond of him more and more and begin to visit him frequently. Obviously, the red is a symbol of protest which the children like and that is what makes Velutha dearer than ever to them.

The procession plays a role in bringing Ammu and Velutha closer too. Ammu knows Velutha from his boyhood days when he used to come with his father to the back entrance of the Ayemenem House and delivered coconuts he had plucked.[67] He made intricate toys for Ammu and brought them to her. Though he was younger than Ammu, he used to call her Ammukutty (Little Ammu).[68] When Rahel recognises Velutha in the procession and shouts unwittingly, Ammu rebukes her because she is conscious of the fact that if Baby Kochamma and Chacko come to know about his political and trade union activities the consequences will be dire.[69] As for herself, the event leads to a happy discovery, the discovery of a kindred, rebellious spirit in Velutha. She hopes that "under his careful cloak of cheerfulness, he housed a living, breathing anger against the smug, ordered world that she so raged against."[70]

Besides the kindred spirit, she finds other qualities in Velutha which attract. Velutha's love for her children is one of the factors. Of course, there is a physical aspect of the attraction too. This is how Ammu discovers a man in him suddenly:

> "A little way away, Velutha walked up the short cut through the rubber trees. Barebodied.... He wore his printed dark blue and black mundu loosely folded up above his knees. On his back, his lucky leaf from the birth mark tree (that made the monsoons come on time)....
>
> ...She wondered at how his body had changed—so quietly, from a flat muscled boy's body into a man's body. Contoured and hard. A swimmer's body. A swimmer-carpenter's body. Polished with a high-wax body polish.
>
> He had high cheekbones and a white, sudden smile.
>
> ...His smile was the only piece of baggage he had carried with him from boyhood to manhood."[71]
>
> Velutha too discovered the woman in Ammu:
>
> In that brief moment, Velutha looked up and saw things that he hadn't seen before....
>
> For instance, he saw that Rahel's mother was a woman. That she had deep dimples when she smiled and that they stayed on long after her smile left her eyes. He saw that her brown arms were round and firm and perfect. That her shoulders shone, but her eyes were somewhere else.... He saw too that he was not necessarily the only

> giver of gifts. That she had gifts to give him too. This knowing slid into him cleanly, like the sharp edge of a knife. Cold and hot at once. It only took a moment.[72]

That is how the "giving" and "taking" of gifts begins, how the mother loves the man at night whom the children love in the day, how the "love laws" are broken—the laws that "lay down who should be loved. And how. And how much."[73]

The rendezvous continues for thirteen nights and then events take an unexpected turn. Velutha's father sees "night after night, a little boat being rowed across the river" and returning "at dawn." He comes to know "what his Untouchable son had touched."[74] So he goes to Mammachi and tells her the "story of a man and woman, standing together in the moonlight. Skin to skin."[75] That provides a golden opportunity to Baby Kochamma to settle her accounts. "She saw it as God's way of punishing Ammu for her sins and simultaneously avenging her (Baby Kochamma's) humiliation at the hands of Velutha and the men in the march—the Modalala Mariakutty taunts, the forced flag-waiving."[76] She goes to the Kottayam Police Station and cooks up a case of attempted rape of Ammu and kidnapping of three children, one of them found dead.[77]

As for Mammachi, she is hardly better in her behaviour to Velutha. She summons Velutha to her house and when he comes unsuspecting, she uses an abusive language that surprises all the listeners. Finally, she screams: "If I find you on my property tomorrow I'll have you castrated like the pariah dog that you are! I'll have you killed!" Velutha replies to that quietly: "We'll see about that" and nothing more. His restraint and good manners present a remarkable contrast to the ill-temper of the sophisticated lady who spits in the face of Velutha.[78]

Now Velutha goes to Comrade Pillai, unaware of the fact that the leader considered him "the only snag" in his plan, "an ally he would rather have done without" and intends to exploit Touchable Workers' irrational resentment for his own benefit.[79] Velutha is also ignorant of Pillai's advice to remove Velutha somehow, an advice that surprised Chacko.[80] So when the naive fellow goes to Pillai he dismisses him with the remark: "But Comrade, you should know that party was not constituted to support workers' indiscipline in their private life."[81] That leaves us wondering whether the party was constituted to defend caste rules and further the ambitions of Pillai. At the Kottayam Police Station, Pillai does not try to challenge false accusation against Velutha and hides the fact that he is a card-holding member of the Communist Party. Thus by denying him the protection of the party, he ensures his end.[82] But there is nothing unusual or unexpected in it. He lives in a society "where a man's death could be more profitable than his life had ever been."[83]

So a posse of Touchable policemen crossed the Meenachal river. They were servants of the state pledged to the virtues of politeness, obedience, loyalty, intelligence, courtesy and efficiency. They went to Kari Saipu's house called the History House in the novel. They woke up Velutha with their boots and beat him severely. Rahel and Estha who were hidden in the same house woke up by the screams and came to know what has happened. Velutha had become semi-conscious and was not moving. "His skull was fractured in three places. His nose and both his cheek-bones were smashed, leaving his face pulpy, undefined.... His spine was damaged in two places, the concussion had paralysed his right arm and resulted in a loss of control over his bladder and rectum. Both his knees were shattered." Still, they brought handcuffs and locked his arms across his back. But they did not fail to make fun of his painted nail before that and one of them flicked at his penis with his stick. As he could not walk, they dragged him to the police station where he died at night.[84]

If that appears inhuman to us, the novelist hastens to inform us what the people in power are sure to say about it: "Unlike the custom of rampaging religious mobs or conquering armies running riot, that morning in the Heart of Darkness the posse of Touchable Policemen acted with economy, not frenzy. Efficiency, not anarchy. Responsibility, not hysteria.... After all, they were not battling an epidemic. They were merely inoculating a community against an outbreak."[85] They were defending social norms, the traditional caste rules, the "love laws" which did not permit a Paravan to love a Syrian Christian.

They had their own defence of what they did and the novelist puts it ironically as follows: "if they hurt Velutha more than they intended to, it was only because any kinship, any connection between themselves and him, any implication that if nothing else, at least biologically he was a fellow creature—had been severed long ago. They were not arresting a man, they were exercising fear."[86] How can one behave well with untouchables if they are believed to be not human beings but animals to be feared?

Most of the critics speak highly about the character of Velutha. Twinkle B. Manavar who has studied him at some length reaches the conclusion: "Velutha stands out as a very tall figure in the novel. It was his desire to 'relive' as a touchable which resulted in the tragedy.... His place is certainly nearer to a Shakespearean tragic hero."[87] K.V. Surendran finds a 'rebel' in Velutha and says: "Velutha, the brave is one of the very well drawn out characters in the novel."[88] Only Vinita Bhatnagar finds fault with Velutha. Always, he is acted upon. Never does he act or question the status quo.... The portrayal of Velutha in Roy's novel is a good example of what happens when an "upper caste Christian" of mixed Bengali Brahmin descent attempts to capture a Dalit life story in literature.[89] The learned critic has her own reasons of dissatisfaction with Arundhati Roy whom she deems anti-communist. Her criticism, however, proves a disservice to the cause she proceeds to serve. Ms. Vinita Bhatnagar has every right to be proud of her pure U.P. Kayasth blood, but is it not a strange kind of Marxism that looks down upon the inter-marriages between religious, linguistic or ethnic groups?

REFERENCES

1. Thapar, Romila, *Ancient Indian Social History,* New Delhi, 1978, 45.
2. Sharma, R.S., *Sudras in Ancient India,* Delhi, 1980, 146.
3. Mukherjee, Prabhati, *Beyond The Four Varnas,* Delhi, 1988, 104.
4. Renfrew, Colin, *Archaeology & Language,* New York, 1988, 188.
5. Shaffer, J.G., The Indo-Aryan invasions: Cultural myth and archaeological reality, *The People of South Asia* (ed. Lucaks, J.R.), New York, 1984, 77-90.
6. Sethna, K.D., *The Problem of Aryan Origins,* Calcutta, 1980 and *Karpasa in Prehistoric India,* Delhi, 1981; Talageri, Shrikant G., *The Aryan Invasion*

Theory: A Reappraisal, Delhi, 1996; Singh, Bhagwan, *The Vedic Harappans,* Delhi, 1996.

7. Ambedkar, B.R., *Who Were the Shudras,* Bombay, 1970, 57-82.
8. Ambedkar, B.R., *The Untouchables,* New Delhi, 1948, 62.
9. *Ibid.,* 155.
10. Roy, U.N., "Origin of Untouchability," published serially (in five chapters) in *Tulsi-Prajna,* the quarterly research journal of Jain Vishvabharati Institute, Ladnun, Rajasthan in Vol. XX, No. 1-2; Vol. XX, No. 4; Vol. XXI, No. 3; Vol. XXII, No. 3 and Vol. XXII, No. 4.
11. Roy, U.N., "When did Untouchability Originate," *Tulsi-Prajna,* Vol. XXI, No. 3, 79-94.
12. *Ibid.,* 83.
13. Sen., K., *Bharatvarsa men jatibheda,* Allahabad, 1952, 6.
14. Chaitanya, Krishna, *Kerala,* New Delhi, 1979, 50.
15. *Ibid.,* 53.
16. *Ibid.,* 54.
17. *Ibid.,* 56-57.
18. Bhatnagar, Vinita, "Fictions of Caste: Dalit Character in the Modern Indian Novel" included in *The Critical Studies of Arundhati Roy's 'The God of Small Things* edited by Dodiya & Chakraborty, New Delhi, 1999, 95.
19. Tharoor, Shashi, *India From Midnight To The Millennium,* New Delhi, 1998, 105-106.
20. *Ibid.,* 69.
21. Roy, Arundhati, *The God of Small Things,* London, 1998, 73-74.
22. *Ibid.,* 13.
23. *Ibid.,* 77.
24. *Ibid.,* 77, 278.
25. *Ibid.,* 73.
26. *Ibid.,* 278.
27. *Ibid.,* 69.
28. *Ibid.,* 66.
29. *Ibid.,* 74.
30. *Ibid.,* 77.
31. *Ibid.,* 76.
32. *Ibid.,* 198-199.
33. *Ibid.,* 76.
34. *Ibid.,* 260-261.
35. *Ibid.,* 76-77.
36. *Ibid.,* 78.
37. *Ibid.,* 76.

38. Roy, Arundhati, *The God of Small Things*, London, 1998, 255.
39. *Ibid.*, 76, 255.
40. *Ibid.*, 255.
41. *Ibid.*, 78.
42. *Ibid.*, 256.
43. *Ibid.*, 255-256.
44. *Ibid.*, 200.
45. Dhawan, R.K. (ed.), *Arundhati Roy The Novelist Extraordinary*, New Delhi, 1999, 222.
46. *Ibid.*, 223.
47. Roy, Arundhati, *op. cit.*, 78.
48. *Ibid.*, 77.
49. *Ibid.*, 206.
50. *Ibid.*, 209, 214.
51. *Ibid.*, 209-211.
52. *Ibid.*, 214.
53. *Ibid.*, 207.
54. *Ibid.*, 207.
55. *Ibid.*, 76.
56. Dodiya & Chakraborty (ed.), *The Critical Studies of Arundhati Roy's The God of Small Things*, New Delhi, 1999, 31-32.
57. Roy, Arundhati, *op.cit.*, 74-76.
58. *Ibid.*, 76-77.
59. *Ibid.*, 77.
60. *Ibid.*
61. *Ibid.*, 69, 71, 73, 81.
62. *Ibid.*, 81.
63. *Ibid.*, 119.
64. *Ibid.*, 73.
65. *Ibid.*, 71.
66. *Ibid.*, 177.
67. *Ibid.*, 73.
68. *Ibid.*, 74.
69. *Ibid.*, 71.
70. *Ibid.*, 176.
71. *Ibid.*, 174-175.
72. *Ibid.*, 176.
73. *Ibid.*, 177.
74. *Ibid.*, 78.
75. *Ibid.*, 235.

76. Roy, Arundhati, *Op. cit.*, 237.
77. *Ibid.*, 259.
78. *Ibid.*, 284.
79. *Ibid.*, 121.
80. *Ibid.*, 278.
81. *Ibid.*, 287.
82. *Ibid.*, 262.
83. *Ibid.*, 281.
84. *Ibid.*, 304-312.
85. *Ibid.*, 309.
86. *Ibid.*
87. Dodiya & Chakraborty, *op. cit.*, 129.
88. *Ibid.*, 70.
89. *Ibid.*, 98.

6

THE ENVIRONMENT IN THE NOVEL

Socially aware intellectuals cannot disregard the environment in the modern world. Arundhati Roy is deeply concerned about it. Her approach is not confined to writing for the environment, she is deeply involved with the agitations concerned with environmental issues like Narmada Bachao Andolan and The Campaign Against Nuclear Weapons in India.

The environment is one of the "small things" neglected for a long time in India. At the time the Constituent Assembly began its deliberations, none of its members cared to utter even a word about the environment. Naturally, therefore, the *Constitution* it produced had nothing to say about it. It was the Forty-second Amendment Act of 1976 that came into effect from January 3, 1977 which inserted Article 48-A in the Constitution. The insertion reads as follows: "The state shall endeavour to protect and improve the environment and to safeguard the forests and wild life of the country."

There has been an awakening in respect of environment during the last three decades nationally and internationally. It has given rise to a number of organisations, including political parties, agitating for issues related to environment in the west. They are generally known as the Greens. In India, such concern has not found an organised expression. Environment is a matter that worries only a few conscious individuals in our country.

Yet the importance of environment for living beings cannot be gainsaid or even underplayed. It is too vital for our survival to be ignored. To put it briefly, the balance of our eco-system is threatened today by wanton destruction of vegetation and wild life on one hand and pollution of different kinds on the other. Destruction of vegetation threatens to stop the supply of the essential things we need like timber, firewood, honey etc. and to deprive a section of our people who depend for their livelihood on forests. It causes soil erosion, floods and drought too. It has already turned certain areas into deserts. A number of animals (cheetah, lion, tiger, black buck deer, one-horned rhinoceros etc.), reptiles (crocodile etc.) and birds (peacock, large falcon etc.) have become rare and endangered. Automobile exhausts smokes from factories, insecticides and herbicides are polluting air and causing diseases like headache, asthma, and lung diseases. Water and soil fare no better as industrialization progresses. Sound pollution is a well-known factor of modern life. It is contributing to the diseases like high blood-pressure, insomnia, nervous diseases and heart ailments. The worst of all is the radioactivity caused by exploding atomic bombs which pollutes air, water and soil and lasts for a very long time. It causes diseases like leucomia, bone tumour, genetic deformity and infant mortality etc.

Awareness of the importance of environment has led to certain activities for conservation. Thus afforestation is encouraged now officially. National Parks and Reserved Forests have been demarcated by state and central governments. Besides special projects to protect crocodiles, tigers, rhinoceros and deers, a number of sanctuaries and national parks have been set up and hunting of rare and endangered wild life has been legally prohibited. Attempts are also being made to prevent the pollution caused by automobile exhausts and industrial units. Courts have moved against sound pollution, though their directions are yet to be followed sincerely and strictly by the people.

Despite all these positive gestures there is much that is wanting. We are a nation proud of religious and cultural heritage. We boast about our sense of higher values, we take a lot of trouble for spiritual gains. We endeavour a lot to make our after-life happy. But we are loath in matters of civic sense and social hygiene. On the other (practical) side of our talk of spiritualism lies our senseless hankering after riches and pursuit of immediate gain. So we make money by destroying vegetation and nature takes a heavy toll for it in the form of soil erosion, land-slide and floods. We build dams, canals, barrages etc. for growing more crops (mostly cash crops) with the hope of getting more electricity, jobs, agricultural products and so on but pay little heed to the flaura and fauna which our projects threaten. Even less consideration is given to the problems of salination of soil and lowering of water-level. Loopholes in the laws to prevent pollution are frequently discovered by the fertile brains of the propertied and exploited to the utmost. Radioactivity, the worst type of pollution, is promoted unwittingly by our patriotic zeal as we aspire to become a strong nation in the world.

Arundhati Roy is not an intellectual, preaching nice things from ivory tower. She has shown her serious commitment by joining like-minded people on vital issues related to environment. It is worthwhile now to discuss her writings and activities in this respect.

Arundhati Roy joined a seminar held on the Hiroshima Day and the paper she presented there appeared as a ten page article in an English weekly *The Outlook* dated Aug. 3, 1998 (62-71). Later it appeared as a booklet published by D.C. Books, Kottayam in October 1998 and was reprinted in November. The copyright of the booklet *The End of Imagination* is held not by Arundhati Roy herself, but by N. Ram, Convenor, the Campaign Against Nuclear Weapons in India. Her activist stance is also seen in her solidarity with the Chaliyar Human Rights Samithi fighting against pollution caused by Grasim industry at Mavoor in Kojhikode, Kerala. She received Dalit Sahitya Academy Award at Calicut on January 15, 1999 and the public address she made on the occasion underlines the same spirit.[1] She is also reported to have opposed "a new development plan for the Panchmarhi area in which hotel-building would be allowed at the cost of despoiling the beauty and sylvan backdrop of" the hill station.[2] Most important of all is her association with the Narmada Bachao Andolan to which she has assigned the royalties of her booklet *The Greater Common Good* published by India Book Distributors, Bombay in 1999. She joined the 14 year old Narmada Bachao Andolan led by the social activist Medha Patekar and journeyed with hundreds of campaigners on an eight-day rally under the banner of 'Free the Narmada Campaign' which ended on August 1999. The rally covered eight hundred kilometres beginning and ending in Indore. Jharna Jhaveri (the filmmaker) and Arundhati Roy were the main speakers at the rally. The rally was organised to draw attention to the immediate prospect of submergence of 50 odd villages in Gujarat, Madhya Pradesh and Maharashtra as a consequence of a Supreme Court order. When the rally halted at Baba Amte's ashram in Kasravad, the veteran Gandhian social worker welcomed it as "the Gangotri of global mobilisation of the intelligentsia" and hoped that "Arundhati will continue to stir the world's conscience."[3]

Such activities are worrying to a section of people, namely, the Central Government, state governments of Madhya Pradesh, Gujarat and Maharashtra and their supporters. So Arundhati Roy is often criticised for developing a social conscience suddenly and joining a convenient band wagon to assuage it. In an interview published in the *Frontline,* she answers her critics quite adequately and brilliantly. "Is it a crime to develop suddenly a social conscience? ...But the critics you mention should take a look at my earlier work—for instance they could begin by reading *The God of Small Things,* or going to the School of Architecture and reading my B. Arch, thesis. They could read back issues of a magazine, called *Urban India,* published by the National Institute of Urban Affairs. They could read back issues of *Sunday,* where I published three essays before I became 'famous.' But then I was criticised for writing what I wrote because I was a 'failed' writer. Now I am criticised because I'm a 'successful' writer."[4] That leaves not much to add. I can only observe that Arundhati Roy could well have become a publicist for the authorities after her success and thereby she could have multiplied her wealth. Political patronage could well have assured her a big chair in some university or the post of an ambassador or High Commissioner. That she chose to become a dissident, a heretic instead speaks volumes for her.

Her essay *The End of Imagination,* mentioned above is her reaction to Pokhran II, the explosion of a nuclear bomb by India in May 1998. She begins by reminding us what the educated generally know but often ignore, the basic truth that a nuclear war is not just like any other war "in which countries battle against countries and men battle men."

"If there is a nuclear war, our foes will not be China or America or even each other. Our foe will be the earth herself. The very elements—the sky, the air, the land, the wind and water—will all turn against us. Their wrath will be terrible.

Our cities and forests, our fields and villages will burn for days. Rivers will turn to poison. The air will become fire. The wind will spread the flames. When everything there is to burn has burned and the fires, the smoke will rise and shut out the sun. The earth will be enveloped in darkness. There will be no day. Only interminable night. Temperatures will drop to far below freezing and nuclear winter will set in. Water into toxic ice. Radioactive fallout will seep through the earth and contaminate ground water. Most living things, animal and vegetable, fish and fowl, will die. Only rats and cockroaches will breed and multiply and compete with foraging, relict humans for what little food there is.

What shall we do then, those of us who are still alive? Burned and blind and bald and ill, carrying the cancerous carcasses of our children in our arms, where shall we go? What shall we eat? What shall we drink? What shall we breathe?[5]

If the above extract seems to be taken from a science fiction, we cannot dismiss it as such. Potentiality of radioactive fallout to contaminate our environment and make it inhabitable for living beings cannot be doubted by anybody who cares to know and think. The questions raised by Arundhati Roy are, therefore, quite relevant and timely.

It is argued, however, that India can survive a nuclear war. The citizens are advised to take the same safety measures as the ones recommended by the scientists in the event of accidents at nuclear plants. The measures include taking iodine pills, consuming only stored water and food, avoiding milk and giving powdered milk to infants etc. To such recommendations, Arundhati Roy retorts: "What do you do with these levels of lunacy? What do you do if you're trapped in an asylum and the doctors are all dangerously deranged?"[6] That sounds too harsh but we can realise the truth it contains from our day to day experience. How accurate the estimates of provisions required for survival are likely to be? How much of them can be stored and supplied to the citizens by the government and non-government agencies? Judging from the functioning of rationing system, of water supply and of the electricity supply, the answers are obvious and far from satisfactory. There is little reason to believe that people who fail in normal times will suddenly turn into efficient ones. Moreover, we cannot but question the propriety of equating a nuclear war with a nuclear accident and concluding that what suffices in the case of the latter will do in the case of the former too. They differ in nature and extent and can be equated only on pain of death and destruction.

There are persons who argue for nuclear weapons as they contend that those weapons deter war. Arundhati Roy demolishes this Theory of Deterrence pointing to two fundamental flaws inherent in it. The first flaw given by her is the following: "It assumes that what deters you (the fear of annihilation) will deter them. What about those who are not deterred by that? The suicide bomber psyche—'We'll take you with us' school—is that an outlandish thought? How did Rajiv Gandhi die?"[7] Then, the vital decisions about nuclear policy are made by governments and we can never be sure about them. The reasons are not far to seek: "Governments change. They wear masks within masks."[8] Secondly, the theory is premised on fear. "But fear is premised on knowledge.... Deterrence will not and can not work given the levels of ignorance and illiteracy that hang over our two countries like dense, impenetrable veils (witness the VHP wanting to distribute radioactive sand from the Pokhran desert as prasad all over India. A cancer yatra?)" Her arguments are too pithy to be dismissed or even challenged and they lead to a conclusion that deserves serious thought: "The Theory of Deterrence is nothing but a perilous joke in a world where iodine pills are prescribed as a prophylactic for nuclear irradiation."[9]

Then she proceeds to persuade us to consider what is likely to happen when numerous countries beside India and Pakistan begin to make nuclear weapons and a market for such weapons develops; "...when it gets truly competitive and prices fall, not just governments, but anybody who can afford it can have their own private arsenal.... There will be a new world order. The dictatorship of the pro- nuke elite."[10] Thus, even without a nuclear war, threats to our environment will remain in the world which continues to make and possess nuclear weapons. And these threats are not limited to our environment, they pass much beyond them as she puts it; "Nuclear weapons pervade our thinking. Control our behaviour. Administer our societies. Inform our dreams."[11] In other words, nuclear weapons threaten not only the environment, they imperil our freedom and social values as well. They are a real danger to sane thinking.

Making a nuclear bomb is generally defended as politically expedient. The three official reasons given for it are "China, Pakistan and Exposing Western Hypocrisy." She examines the reasons and finds them far from satisfactory.[12] As we have to confine ourselves to her concern for environment, we refrain from quoting them. She is undoubtedly justified in holding that India's problems "cannot and will not be solved by pointing nuclear missiles at Pakistan." Even her bitter enemies dare not question the wisdom of her argument when she writes: "Though we are separate countries, we share skies, we share winds, we share water. Where radioactive fallout will land on any given day depends on the direction of the wind and rain. Lahore and Amritsar are thirty miles apart. If we bomb Lahore, Punjab will burn. If we bomb Karachi—then Gujarat and Rajasthan, perhaps even Bombay, will burn. Any nuclear war with Pakistan will be a war against ourselves."[13]

Her other booklet *The Greater Common Good* contains something which reminds us of her novel *The God of Small Things:* "...We have to fight our specific wars in specific ways. Who knows, perhaps that's what the twenty first century has in store for us. The dismantling of the Big. Big bombs, big dams, big ideologies, big contradictions, big countries, big wars, big heroes, big mistakes. Perhaps it will be the Century of the Small."[14]

Arundhati Roy informs us that there are 3600 big dams in India, 3300 of them were built after 1947. One thousand more are under construction. "Yet one fifth of our population—200 million people—does not" have safe drinking water and two-thirds—600 million-lack basic sanitation. India goes on building big dams when they are "being de-commissioned, blown up" in the First World. She is opposed to big dams because they are "a brazen means of taking water, land and irrigation away from the poor and gifting it to the rich." Secondly, they make many people homeless and destitute. Last but not the least, they are indefensible ecologically. "They lay the earth to waste. They cause floods, water-logging, salinity, they spread disease. There is mounting evidence that links Big Dams to earthquakes.... They last only as long as it takes Nature to fill them with silt."[16]

There are other bitter truths she presents to us. Thus, we learn that after spending Rs. 87,000 crores on the irrigation sector alone during the last fifty years, India has "more drought-prone areas and more flood-prone areas today than there were in 1947."[17] We also learn that though there are no official statistics on people displaced by big dams, the figure cannot be less than 50 million. She points out that "in 1995 state granaries were overflowing with 30 million tonnes of unsold grain" but "at the same time, forty per cent of India's population—more than 350 million people—were living below the poverty line" which means they were unable to buy food. While people died of starvation in Kalahandi in 1996, "rice production in Kalahandi was higher than the national average! Rice was exported from Kalahandi District to the Centre."[18] So she goes on to reject the myth that India lives in villages and declares: "India lives in her cities. India's villages have only to serve her cities."[19]

Arundhali Roy opposes the projects to build big dams in the Narmada valley both on the considerations of the adverse effect it will have on the environment as well as the misery it will definitely bring to many. The Narmada Valley Development Project, she informs us, "will alter the ecology of the entire river basin of one of India's biggest rivers. For better or for worse, it will affect the lives of twenty-five million people who live in the valley. It will submerge and destroy 4000 square kilometres of natural deciduous forest."[20] Its impact on the environment and the people living along the valley is already severe. "Around the dam site and the nearby villages, the number of cases of malaria has increased six-fold." Several kilometres upstream from the Sardar Sarovar Dam, huge deposits of silts has cut off the access to the river which compels women to walk miles with their water pots and cows and goats are getting stranded and dying. Further upstream, the poor used to cultivate rice, melons, cucumbers and gourds on the rich, shallow silt banks in the dry months. Now the water from the Bargi dam is released without warning and "their crops washed away, leaving them with no livelihood."[21]

Alluding to the fanatics who destroyed the mosque in Ayodhya (in 1992), Arundhati Roy questions the propriety of "destroying the sacred hills and groves, the places of worship, the ancient homes of the gods and demons of tribal people," "of submerging a valley that has yielded fossils, microliths and rock paintings, the only valley in India, according to archaeologists, that contains an uninterrupted record of human occupation from the Old Stone Age."[22] Her questions are quite valid and difficult to answer for people who talk so much about the heritage of India.

We cannot but appreciate her concern for the loss of bio-diversity and wildlife habitat when she writes: "The Sardar Sarovar Reservoir, when the dam reaches its full height, is going to submerge about 13,000 hectares of prime forest land.... Between the Narmada Sagar dam and the Sardar Sarovar dam, 50,000 hectares of old growth broad leaved forest will be submerged—To mitigate this loss, the Government decided to expand the Shoolpaneshwar Wildlife Sanctuary near the dam, south of the river. There is a hare brained scheme that envisages drowning animals from the submerged forests swimming their way to wild-life corridors that will be created for them and setting up home in the New! Improved! Shoolpaneshwar Sanctuary."[23]

She draws our attention to the fact that the dam is going to destroy the Hilsa fish of the Narmada estuary in Bharuch which produces 13,000 tonnes of Hilsa and fresh water prawn and deprive 40,000 fisher folk of their livelihood. There is no way to make good of the loss because "so far, scientists have not managed to breed Hilsa artificially. The rearing of Hilsa depends on getting spawn from wild adults, which will in all likelihood be eliminated by the dam. Dams have either eliminated or endangered one-fifth of the world's fresh water fish."[24]

Arundhati Roy explodes our widely held notions about the benefits of canal irrigation when she declares: "Perennial irrigation does to soil roughly that anabolic steroids do to the human body." Traditional subsistence crops that need less water yield place to cash crops that need more water. That disturbs the normal living of the people and overtimes makes the soil "too poor to support the extra demands made on it. Gradually, in the way a steroid-using athlete becomes an invalid, the soil becomes depleted and degraded, and agricultural yields begin to decrease."[25] Then she reveals the fact that "land irrigated by well water is today almost twice as productive as land irrigated by canals" while the estimates about salinized and water-logged land in India "vary between 6 and 10 million hectares."[26]

Referring to the secret Government studies, she informs us that "more than 52% of the Sardar Sarovar Command area is prone to water-logging and salinization."[27] As canals block the flow of the natural, seasonal water and lead to water-logging, it becomes necessary to build an alternate, artificial drainage system in conjunction with the canals. But the dam builders exclude it from their ambitious irrigation projects because the cost is simply prohibitive and makes the projects unviable. "It costs five times as much to provide adequate drainage as it does to irrigate the same amount of land." That is why they have excluded drainage from their plans too. It means permitting salinization and water-logging to devastate land and then to seek fresh loans from World Bank and other agencies. That is what has happened in other countries and that is what is going to happen in India too.[28]

As for the supposed benefits of the project, there is little reason to believe them. First of all, actual observed flow data for the Narmada during 1948-1992 showed that the river yielded only 22.69 MAF (million acre feet) water which was 18 per cent less than the assumed figure of 27.22 MAF extrapolated in 1969.[29] The hope of getting 1450 megawatts of power is belied by the harsh reality. The purposes of multi-purpose dams conflict with each other. "Irrigation uses up the water you need to produce power. Flood control requires you to keep the reservoir empty during the monsoon months.... And this defeats the purpose of irrigation, which is to store the monsoon water.... The result of all these mutually conflicting aims, studies say, is that when the Sardar Sarovar Projects are completed and the scheme is fully functional, it will end up producing only 3% of the power that its planners say it will. About 50 megawatts. And if you take into account the power needed to pump water through its vast network of canals, the Sardar Sarovar projects will end up consuming more electricity than they produce."[30]

Even in terms of human suffering, the projects deserve no support. Official estimates of the people it will displace have varied from year to year but the Narmada Bachao Andolan places the figure at about half a million.[31] Most of the project affected people are excluded from government estimates on technical grounds. Even when their claims are admitted, they fare hardly better. The Government of Gujarat boasts of its rehabilitation policy and offers to resettle not only its own displaced persons but those from Madhya Pradesh and Maharashtra as well. In practice, it has not "even managed to rehabilitate people from its own 19 villages slated for submergence, let alone the rest of the 226 villages in the other two states."[32] The so-called resettlement proves a cruel joke, when in several resettlement sites, people are "dumped in rows of corrugated tinsheds which are furnaces in summer and fridges in winter. Some of them are located in dry river beds which, during the monsoon, turn into fast-flowing drifts."[33] Malaria, diarrhoea and other diseases are taking a toll everyday in these sites.[34] Then the displaced persons, mostly tribals and dalits, have lost their forest, their river and their livestock which kept them alive. They are destitutes now striving to earn a living as wage-labourers.[35] Such things have happened and will continue to happen as the recommendations of the Morse Report[36] as well as those of the Five Member Group[37] were disregarded.

The Greater Common Good was criticised by people accustomed to viewing big dams as the instruments of progress. Gail Omvedt found noting but 'rhetoric' and 'eco-romanticism' in it. Arundhati Roy gave her a befitting reply: "Gail Omvedt subscribes to the classic 'green revolution' school of thought—maximum production in a minimum period of time regardless of ecological consequences. Long-term sustainabilily is not taken into consideration. Thousand of hectares of land are now water-logged and salt-affected thanks to this approach. It's the steroid-user syndrome. If avoiding steroids is romantic then perhaps I am a romantic.... We must stop pretending that rehabilitation is possible. It is'nt. In the last 15 years not one village in the submergence zone has been rehabilitated."[38] Indeed if one intends to seek romantics, one must seek them in the ranks of the enthusiastic supporters of big dams that destroy vegetation and wildlife, devastate land and bring displacement and destitution for purposes which are never likely to be realised.

Eco-conscious as the novelist is, her concern for the environment finds an adequate expression in *The God of Small Things*. Jason Cawley, one of the five Booker judges writes, "Roy's achievement...is never to forget about small things in life, insects and flowers, wind and water, the outcaste and despised."[39] We have discussed her commitment to "the outcaste and despised" in the previous chapter. So we now come to the other small things in life, namely, "insects and flowers, wind and water" which stand for the environment: The novel lays bare how our environment is being subjected to decay and destruction and points out the reasons that lie behind it too.

We can begin with the river Meenachal. Estha and Rahel dreamt of the river in their childhood. They had reason to do so:

> It was warm, the water. Grey green. Like rippled silk. With fish in it. With the sky and trees in it. And at night, the broken yellow moon in it.[40]

As an object of beauty it seemed a joy for ever. When Rahel returned twenty-three years later, the river "greeted her with a ghastly skull's smile, with holes where teeth had been and a limp hand raised from a hospital bed." Though it was June and raining, "the river was no more than a swollen drain now. A thin ribbon of thick water that lapped wearily at the mud banks on either side, sequinned with the occasional silver of a dead fish. It was choked with a succulent weed, whose furred brown roots waved like thin tentacles under water. Bronze-winged lily-trotters walked across it. Splay-footed, cautious." The river was no more than "a slow, slugging green ribbon lawn that ferried garbage to the sea" now.[41] Estha too found that the river "smelled of shit, and pesticides bought with World Bank loans. Most of the fish had died. The ones that survived suffered from fin-rot and had broken out in boils."[42]

Shit and pesticides are the two sources of pollution mentioned here. As for the shit, children of the shanty hutments on the other side of the river defecating on the river bed may be responsible for it. The water of the river is used for washing clothes and pots too upstream and receives "unadulterated factory effluents" as well. Little wonder then that in summer, "the shit lifted off the river and hovered over Ayemenem like a hot."[43] Such a disaster could have been avoided had people stopped short of demanding more from the river than it could give. But the blind pursuit of immediate gain, called the steroid syndrome by Arundhati Roy elsewhere, left no room for sane thought: "Down river, a salt water barrage had been built, in exchange for votes from the influential paddy-farmer lobby. The barrage regulated the inflow of salt water from the back waters that opened into the Arabian Sea. So now they had two harvests a year instead of one. More rice, for the price of a river."[44] Thus we find that it is not wisdom or science that prevails but the votes and lobbies that control them, have the decisive voice in our society.

The river is not the only sufferer in the novel. The village Ayemenem once known for freshness, matchless greenery and rural quietness has changed when Rahel returns to it. Its population has "swelled to the size of a little town." There is only a "fragile facade of greenery" left now and only the houses nestled under trees along unmotorable narrow paths that branch off the main road give the village "a semblance of rural quietness." Otherwise people can gather at a moment's notice to beat to death a careless bus driver or to smash the windscreen of a car that dares to venture out on the day of an Opposition bandh.[45] Estha finds "the new, freshly baked, iced, Gulf-money houses built by nurses, masons, wire benders and bank clerks who worked hard and unhappily in far away places."[46] To give a real Indian touch to the process of urbanization "small fish appear in the puddles that fill the PWD potholes on the highways."[47]

The estate of Karri Saipu, also known as History House, has changed too. It is renovated and painted now, a five star hotel called 'Heritage.' The locality is described as 'God's Own Country' in hotel brochures. But what is the reality about it? "The view from the hotel was beautiful, but here too the water was thick and toxic. *No Swimming* signs had been put up in stylish calligraphy. They had built a wall to screen off the slum and prevent it from encroaching on Kari Saipu's estate. There wasn't much they could do about the smell...they knew, those clever Hotel People, that smelliness, like other people's poverty, was merely a matter of getting used to."[48] Thus money is being spent to bring more money in lieu of pleasure and comfort for a few who can afford and not to make the locality hygienic for all.

The Ayemenem House, a "grand old house" which saw the rise and fall of five generations has also gone to the dogs. Rahel finds it in a miserable condition:

> "The walls, streaked with moss, had grown soft, and bulged a little with dampness that seeped up from the ground. The wild overgrown garden was full of the whisper and scurry of small lives. In the undergrowth a rat snake rubbed itself against a glistening stone. Hopeful yellow bull frogs cruised the scummy pond for mates. A drenched mongoose flashed across the leaf-strewn drive way.
>
> The house itself looked empty. The doors and windows were locked. The front verandah was bare. Unfurnished."[49]

That is what we read in the opening chapter of the novel. The third chapter contains more details of the same kind:

> "Filth had laid siege to the Ayemenem House like a medieval army advancing on an enemy castle. It clotted every crevice and clung to the window panes.
>
> Midges whizzed in teapots. Dead insects lay in empty vases.
>
> The floor was sticky. White walls had turned an uneven grey. Brass hinges and doorhandles were dull and greasy to the touch. Infrequently used plug points were clogged

> with grime. Light bulbs had a film of oil on them. The only things that shone were the giant cockroaches that scurried around like varnished gofers on a film set."[50]

The skyblue Plymouth was the proud possession of Pappachi in his life. He had bought it from an old Englishman in Munnar and did not allow his wife or anyone else in the family to use it, or even sit in it.[51] When he died, Chacko used it and after Chacko's departure to Canada, Baby Kochamma maintained it for years. But then she became addicted to television and discarded the Plymouth as well as ornamental garden. So this is what happened to the car:

> "With every monsoon, the old car settled more firmly into the ground. Like an angular arthritic hen setting stiffly on her clutch of eggs. With no intention of ever getting up, grass grew around its flat tyres. The Paradise Pickles and Preserves signboard rotted and fell in wards like a collapsed crown."[52] Estha saw a dead sparrow on its back seat.[53]

The factory was the other proud possession of the Ipe family. Rahel finds it no better when she returns to Ayemenem after twenty-three years:

> ...she noticed that one of the gauze doors of the factory had come off its hinges and was popped against the door way. She moved it aside and stepped in. The air was heavy with moisture, wet enough for fish to swim in.
>
> The floor under her shoes was slick with monsoon scum. A small, anxious bat flitted between the roof beams.
>
> The low cement pickle vats silhouetted in the gloom made the factory floor look like an indoor cemetery for tire cylindrical dead.
>
> The earthly remains of Paradise Pickles & Preserves.[54]

Thus, Ayemenem in general and Ayemenem House in particular presents a dismal scene of pollution and decay. The reasons are the same in every case: a callousness toward other living beings and inanimate things and senseless pursuit of immediate gain. People want money and more money, and that right now. They seek comfort and pleasure for the present and do not care for the future. They hanker after riches but do not bother about the consequences. They deprive and cheat others to acquire what they themselves cannot keep and maintain. They refuse to share with others what they have to leave at last to rot. That is the most irrational thing about the behaviour of the civilized in our age and Arundhati Roy brings home the point well in the novel.

REFERENCES

1. Dodiya and Chakraborty (ed.), *The Critical Studies of Arundhati Roy's The God of Small Things,* New Delhi, 1999, 26.
2. *India Today,* July 12,1999, 44.
3. *Frontline,* Aug. 27, 1999, 129-132.
4. *Frontline,* Aug. 27, 1999, 133.
5. Roy, Arundhati, *The End of Imagination,* Kottayam, Nov. 1998, 12-13.
6. *Ibid.,* 14.
7. *Ibid.,* 15-16.
8. *Ibid.,* 16.
9. *Ibid.,* 17.
10. *Ibid.,* 18.
11. *Ibid.*
12. *Ibid.,* 34-37.
13. *Ibid.,* 34.
14. Roy, Arundhati, *The Greater Common Good,* Bombay, 1999, 5.
15. *Ibid.,* 7.
16. *Ibid.,* 8.
17. *Ibid.*
18. *Ibid.,* 13.
19. *Ibid.,* 15.
20. *Ibid.,* 18.
21. *Ibid.,* 34-35.
22. *Ibid.,* 46-47.
23. *Ibid.,* 48.
24. *Ibid.,* 50.
25. *Ibid.,* 51.
26. *Ibid.,* 52.
27. *Ibid.*
28. *Ibid.,* 53.
29. *Ibid.,* 17.
30. *Ibid.,* 23.

31. Roy, Arundhati, *The Greater Common Good*, Bombay, 1999, 22.
32. *Ibid.*, 36.
33. *Ibid.*, 37.
34. *Ibid.*, 38.
35. *Ibid.*
36. *Ibid.*, 31.
37. *Ibid.*, 33.
38. *Frontline*, Aug. 27, 1999, 133.
39. Cowley, Jason, "Why We Chose Arundhati," *India Today*, October 27, 1997, 28.
40. Roy, Arundhati, *The God of Small Things*, London, 1998, 123.
41. *Ibid.*, 124.
42. *Ibid.*, 13.
43. *Ibid.*, 125.
44. *Ibid.*, 124.
45. *Ibid.*, 128.
46. *Ibid.*, 13.
47. *Ibid.*, 1.
48. *Ibid.*, 125-126.
49. *Ibid.*, 1-2.
50. *Ibid.*, 88.
51. *Ibid.*, 48.
52. *Ibid.*, 295.
53. *Ibid.*, 296.
54. *Ibid.*, 192.

CONCLUSION

Every committed writer seeks to change the world around oneself. That requires an ideal or vision of a better society or a better world. Most of these committed writers subscribe to one or other of the prevalent political or philosophical trends like Gandhism, Marxism etc. Arundhati Roy as a committed writer is no exception to that rule. But as our study seems to indicate, she does not subscribe to the conventional views. She is a non-conformist who cannot be identified with one or other trend without certain reservations. She has a world-view of her own, she wants a saner world based on reason which permits individual freedom, takes due regard of natural instincts and shuns violence. Not ruthless pursuits of money and power, but the concern for peace, happiness and equality shall be the guiding factor in the better world she seeks and not force, but persuasion will be the means to achieve the goal.

As I have tried to show in my discussion of her life and her novel, she is a woman of vision and imagination speaking forcibly about certain convictions. It is clear that Arundhati Roy believes in the equality of the sexes. She resents discrimination against women in respect of education, job and property. Though she is close to Gandhians in her faith on non-violence, her views on sex seem not much different from the Bolsheviks. Writing in 1923, Grigorii Batkis, Director of the Moscow Institute of Sexual Hygiene explained in his book, *The Sexual Revolution in Russia*: "Soviet legislation bases itself on the following principle: it declares absolute non-interference of the state and society into sexual matters so long as nobody is injured and no one's interests are encroached upon.... All forms of sexual intercourse are private matters." She believes that society or state has no business to interfere when the sexual relations are based on equality and consent.

That is what she seems to hint at when she describes Rahel breaking the greatest taboo imposed by society, namely, incest.

In social relations, including sex relations, she has no regard for barriers like religion, language, ethnic group, caste or class. It is not without some significance that Arundhati's women ignore such barriers. Margaret marries an Indian, while Rahel marries an American. Ammu marries a Bengali Hindu and later loves a working class Paravan. Nobody ought to be deprived of opportunity, education, job or property on such considerations. Abilities must be rewarded, remunerated and appreciated with least regard to such differences. Every reader of the novel feels resentful of the fact that the abilities of Velutha, even though recognised are not duly appreciated by his employers and even his party pays no attention to them. Equality cannot be achieved by practising and perpetuating inequality nor by resorting to all the means possible for preserving one's supremacy and privileges. As we read the novel, we wonder how untouchability can be abolished de facto if intellectuals like Chacko and communist leaders like Pillai continue to practise it. Similarly we question the use of separate schools for the untouchables.

Children deserve a better treatment in society. Adults must try to understand them and their needs—physical, material, emotional—and impart them good education. Society has to provide them suitable, favourable conditions for their growth and development. The gap between the adults and children ought to be bridged by understanding, sympathy and attention. Problems like child abuse and child labour deserve more attention of our society and laws enacted to defend their interest must be enforced seriously.

The necessity to be attentive to the problems of environment cannot be taken lightly any more. The basic fault of social behaviour has been so far to pursue the immediate gain and paying no heed to dangers lying ahead. Whether it is the question of building dams and canals or growing cash crops, people think about the money they will get soon. Even the governments that prepare and stock weapons are guided by the consideration that the popular sentiment will prolong their days in office. Sanity, however, demands a nuclear-free world that does not permit pollution of any kind. Nothing that threatens our wildlife and vegetation and contaminates our soil, water and air can be permitted to continue.

True, it is difficult to achieve this but that is what can ensure health, happiness and prosperity to mankind and bring peace to the world. May her vision of a sane world materialise!

BIBLIOGRAPHY

Primary Sources

Roy, Arundhati, *The God of Small Things,* London, 1998.

——, *The End of Imagination,* Kottayam, 1998.

——, *The Greater Common Good,* Bombay, 1999.

Others

Anand, Mulk Raj, *Untouchables,* Bombay, 1944.

——, *Two Leaves and A Bud,* Bombay, 1951.

——, *Coolie,* New Delhi, 1981.

Bhattacharya, Bhabani, *So Many Hungers,* New Delhi, 1978.

——, *Music for Mohini,* New Delhi, 1952.

——, *He Who Rides A Tiger,* Bombay, 1954.

Deshpande, Shashi, *The Dark Holds No Terrors,* New Delhi, 1980.

——, *Roots and Shadows,* Bombay, 1983.

——, *That Long Silence,* New Delhi, 1988.

Dr. Amarinder, *Lajo,* New Delhi, 1990

Singh, Khushwant, *Train to Pakistan,* Delhi, 1988.

——, *I Shall Not Hear The Nightingle,* Delhi, 1961.

Secondary Sources

On Roy, Arundhati

Bhatt, Indira and Nityanandam, Indira (ed.), *Explorations: Arundhati Roy's The God of Small Things,* New Delhi, 1999.

Chakravarty, Jaya and Dodiya, Joydip Singh (ed.), *The Critical Studies of Arundhati Roy's The God of Small Things,* New Delhi, 1999.

Dhawan, R.K. (ed.), *Arundhati Roy The Novelist Extraordinary,* New Delhi, 1999.

Sharma, R.S. and Talwar, *Shashibala, Arundhati Roy's The God of Small Things: Critique and Commentary,* New Delhi, 1998.

On others

Cowasjee, Saros, *So Many Freedoms: A Study of the Major Fiction of Mulk Raj Anand,* Madras, 1977.

Fisher, Merlene, *The Wisdom of the Heart: A Study of the Works of Mulk Raj Anand,* New Delhi, 1985.

Gupta, G.S. Balram, *Mulk Raj Anand: A Study of His Fiction in Humanist Perspective,* Bareilly, 1974.

Iyengar, K.R.S., *Indian Writing in English,* New Delhi, 1999.

Parameshwaran, Uma, *A Study of Representative Indo-English Novelists,* New Delhi, 1976.

Pathak, R.S., *The Fiction of Shashi Deshpande,* New Delhi, 2000.

Rajan, P.K., *Mulk Raj Anand: A Revaluation,* New Delhi, 1995.

Sahane, Vasant A., *Khushwant Singh,* New York, 1972.

Sharma, K.K. (ed.), *Perspectives On Mulk Raj Anand,* Ghaziabad, 1978.

Sorot, Balram S., *The Novels of Bhabani Bhattacharya,* New Delhi, 2000.

Walsh, William, *Indian Literature in English,* London, 1990.

Miscellaneous

Agnes, Flavia, *State, Gender and the Rhetoric of Law Reform,* Bombay, 1995.

Ambedkar, B.R., *Who Were the Shudras,* Bombay, 1970.

——, *The Untouchables,* New Delhi, 1948.

Batkis, Grigorii, *The Sexual Revolution in Russia,* Moscow, 1923.

Beauvoir, Simon de, *The Second Sex,* New York, 1964.

Briffault, Robert, *The Mothers: A Study of the Origins of the Sentiments and Institutions,* New York, 1952.

Bullough, Vern, *The Subordinate Sex: A History of Attitudes Toward Women,* New York, 1973.

Chaitanya, Krishna, *Kerala,* New Delhi, 1972.

Foucault, Michael, *The History of Sexuality: An Introduction,* New York, 1978.

Freud, Sigmund, *Totem and Taboo,* New York, 1946.

——, *A General Introduction to Psycho-analysis,* New York, 1960.

Fromm, Eric, *Escape from Freedom,* New York, 1969.

Gupta, Monika (ed.), *Women Writers In The Twentieth Century,* New Delhi, 2000.

Hardgrave, R.L., *Essays In Political Sociology of South India,* New Delhi, 1979.

Hastings, James, *Encyclopedia of Religion and Ethics* (12 Vols.), New York, 1908-21.

Krishnaraj, Maithreyi (ed.), *Women and Violence: A Country Report,* Bombay, 1991.

Kudchedkar, Sirin and Al-Issa, Sabiha (ed.), *Violence Against Women, Women Against Violence,* Delhi, 1998.

Laddle, Joanna and Joshi, Rama, *Daughters of Independence: Gender, Caste, Class in India,* New Delhi, 1986.

Mies, Maria, *Indian Women and Patriarchy,* New Delhi, 1980.

Millet, Kate, *Sexual Politics,* London, 1969.

Milligan, James, *Violence: Reflections on a National Epidemic,* New York, 1996.

Morgan, Robin, *The Anatomy of Freedom: Feminism, Physics and Global Politics,* New York, 1996.

Mukherjee, Prabhati, *Beyond the Four Varnas,* Delhi, 1988.

Naik, J.P., *Elementary Education in India: A Promise to Keep,* Bombay, 1975.

Namboodripad, E.M.S., *Kerala: Yesterday, Today and Tomorrow,* Calcutta, 1968.

Nossiter, T.J., *Communism in Kerala,* Calcutta, 1982.

Reed, Evelyn, *The Women's Involution,* New York, 1975.

——, *Problems of Women's Liberation,* New York, 1975

Renfrew, Colin, *Archaeology and Language,* New York, 1988.

Sartre, J.P., *Existentialism and Humanism,* London, 1952.

Sen, Kshitimohan, *Bharatvarsa men jatibheda* (Hindi), Allahabad, 1952.

Sethna, K.D., *The Problem of Aryan Origin,* Calcutta, 1980.

——, *Karpasa in Pre-historic India,* Delhi, 1981.

Sharma, R.S., *Sudras in Ancient India,* Delhi, 1980.

Shastri, Shakuntala Rao, *Women in the Sacred Laws,* Bombay, 1959.

Shepard, D.L., *The Science of Human Behaviour,* Chicago, 1977.

Singh, Bhagwan, *The Vedic Harrapans,* Delhi, 1996.

Singh, Sushila (ed.), *Feminism and Recent Fiction in English,* New Delhi, 1991.

Smith, W. Robertson, *The Religion of the Semites,* London, 1927.

Spivak, Gayatri Chakravarty, *In Other Worlds: Essays in Cultural Politics,* New York, 1987.

Talageri, Shrikant G., *The Aryan Invasion Theory: A Reappraisal,* Delhi, 1996.

Thapar, Romila, *Ancient Indian Social History,* New Delhi, 1978.

Tharoor, Shashi, *India From Midnight To Millennium,* New Delhi, 1998.

Weiner, Myron, *The Child And The State In India,* New Jersey, 1991.

Winternitz, M., *A History of Indian Literature,* Pune, 1972.

NEWPAPERS AND MAGAZINES

English

Frontline

General Knowledge Today

India Today

Liberation

Outlook

Social Welfare

Sunday

The Literary Criterion

The Hindustan Times

The Hindu

The Week

Women and Revolution (New York)

Bengali

Ananda Bazar Patrika

Dainik Basumati

Desh

Ekus Shatake Narir Adhikar

Bilingual (Hindi-English)

Tulasi-Prajna.